Business School

Book 2

An introduction to human resource management in business

Written by Diane Preston

The Open University Walton Hall, Milton Keynes MK7 6AA

First published 2006. Second edition 2007. Third edition 2010. Fourth edition 2011.

Edited and designed by The Open University.

Printed and bound in the United Kingdom by Charlesworth Press, Wakefield.

ISBN 978 1 8487 3587 3

4.1

Contents

Introduction to Book 2

Welcome to Book 2 of B120, which is an introduction to human resource management (HRM) in business. In this book we explore the business function of HRM and the activities with which it is concerned. We also consider the more difficult questions of what motivates people to go to work in the first place and how a business can create a working environment that motivates people to want to work there. We introduce some of the methods and ideas behind different HRM policies, such as recruitment, appraisal and rewards. We also look at how the concept of HRM has developed over the last few decades to represent, at least theoretically, a different way of thinking about managing people at work. This development reflects not only employees' changing expectations, but also the need for a modern business to be flexible enough to cope with a volatile business environment.

We cannot stress enough the importance of the other B120 resources. The additional activities and learning points in the Study Companion are designed as an integral part of your learning and understanding, and you should now be using your online tutor group forum (TGF) regularly and making contributions as necessary. Study hours for these resources have been calculated as a part of your study of this book.

Aims and objectives

The aims of Book 2 are to:

- consider some definitions of HRM;
- identify the factors that motivate people to want to work for a specific business;
- explore some theories about motivation at work and how an apparent lack of motivation might be managed;
- understand the concept of work design by exploring, first, the job characteristics model and, second, two approaches to work design: Taylorism and the socio-technical approach;
- outline the issues and methods involved in the recruitment, selection, induction and socialisation of employees into a business;
- explain the ways in which individual performance can be assessed, monitored and developed at work;
- understand some of the key theories underpinning these HRM issues;
- provide an appreciation of the function of HRM in a wider context.

Structure

Book 2 is divided into five study sessions:

Session 1	explores an often overlooked aspect of human resource management (HRM): what motivates people to go to work in the first place? Aside from money, there are many theories about what motivates people, the expectations they have and the type of employment or psychological contract that exists between employer and employee. We also look at some of the theory regarding what makes employees stay away from work: that is, absenteeism.
Session 2	looks at the different methods and HRM policies that can be used to structure work and thus increase job satisfaction. The scientific management and socio-technical approaches are compared.
Session 3	outlines the methods used in and the issues to consider in the entry stage of HRM: how to attract and select the right people with the right skills for the business and help them fit in.
Session 4	focuses on performance management, a key concern of any HRM department. Policies are needed within the business so that people know the criteria or standards against which they are being assessed. Providing training and development for employees is an associated part of performance development. We end this study session by looking at some of the methods that can be utilised to help individuals obtain a better understanding of their role in the business, which usually leads to higher motivation levels.
Session 5	attempts to take a step backwards and to look at HRM in a wider context. We explore the standards produced by the professional body of HRM in the UK, the Chartered Institute of Personnel and Development. We consider issues that arise when HRM is left with specialists in the business and when responsibility for people matters is devolved to all line managers. This study session introduces a number of academic models of HRM and notes how they differ. Finally, we look at some of the less considered aspects of HRM: whether strategic integration into the business is possible; the ethical dimension; the idea of 'mischief' at work; and HRM from an insider's point of view.

Where human resource management comes from

Human resource management (HRM) has been defined as:

> A philosophy of people management based on the belief that human resources are uniquely important to sustained business success. An organisation gains competitive advantage by using its people effectively, drawing on their expertise and ingenuity to meet clearly defined objectives.

(Price, 2004, p. 35)

The HRM function has its roots in the changing work conditions of the industrial revolution at the end of the nineteenth century. At that time managing people was about how to get the maximum effort and levels of production out of each person at minimum cost. Any thoughts of people feeling commitment to the business they worked for, and vice versa, were not considered. The development of welfare management was augmented by social commentators such as Charles Dickens whose descriptions of working lives highlighted the need to improve the working conditions of employees and provide some sort of support for them if they were unable to work. As welfare policies and work procedures developed, so a business function concerned with the people side of business was born. This was the welfare function which became known as 'personnel management'.

In more recent times, *personnel management* (the name still used in some businesses) gained a rather negative image. 'Personnel' was often associated with a department full of 'pen-pushers' whose main responsibilities were filling in forms and devising ways of measuring people's productivity. The 'old' personnel function was often peripheral, staffed by specialists and offering a range of people-management services, but rarely central to business strategy. One of the main differences with HRM, it is argued, is that it is directly linked to, and driven by, the objectives of the business.

Business issues are always permeated with HRM concerns. For example, the innovation and new production processes on which the growth of a business depends are reliant on people's knowledge, skills, creativity and ability to change. People *are* the business; without them it is just a set of buildings and machinery.

Why work?

The first study session of this book raises the question of why anyone would want to work. If they are not going to benefit directly, in the way that the owners and stakeholders do, from business profits, what is in it for them? This is an important question for any business and the challenge facing HRM. To end this Introduction we want to raise two key points about managing people, which you should reflect on before and after your study of this book:

1 Organising the efforts of people at work, while also attempting to reinforce their interest and understanding of what is required, is an extremely complex process.

2 While it is important that we know about HRM processes and techniques, it is always healthy for us to retain a note of cynicism about why and whether a business really would want to empower and involve people in the way often advocated in the HRM literature.

As businesses have changed over the past century, so have the people who work within them. Our views about work and what we expect to get from it are very different from those of our predecessors. Before thinking about ways to try to manage people at work, we will now consider the reverse side of the problem: why would people go to work in the first place?

Session 1 Why do people go to work?

Why are we studying the question 'why do people go to work?'? Apart from financial necessity, there are many other reasons why people go to work. Happy, motivated employees are a key component in a successful business. Understanding what motivates people and what to do to increase motivation is a major area of research in both psychology and business studies.

The **aims and objectives** of Session 1 are to:

- introduce the concept of motivation;
- explore the reasons, apart from money, why people might go to work;
- describe some of the key theories which have influenced thinking about motivation at work;
- highlight the changing expectations of both employees and employers within a modern business;
- explain the notion of a psychological contract.

1.1 What motivates people to work?

We will start this study session with a simple activity to get you thinking about work.

Activity 1.1

Spend about **10 minutes** on this activity

Purpose: to think through the different reasons why people might go to work.

Task: make a list of the benefits to be gained by you or anyone else from going to work.

Feedback

Most people go to work to earn money to secure a reasonable standard of living for themselves and their family. How much the job pays will always be an issue, but there are other, non-financial reasons that people may take into account. You will have several on your own list; the ones we thought of are shown in the list below.

Why people might go to work

Non-financial reasons why people choose to go to work might include:

- Job satisfaction: some people will be prepared to earn less if they think that the job is interesting, offers good holidays and benefits, has convenient working hours, and so on.

- Going to work is a good way of meeting people and making friends: an effort is usually made, even if only informally, to create social occasions among people who work together – the infamous Christmas office party, for example!

- Other people's perception of us and our own self-esteem is often affected by the job that we do. When you meet an accountant or an academic, for example, you are likely to make several assumptions about them.

- Work can give people an identity: we feel as though we belong to a group of people, whether as a member of a particular business or of a wider profession, such as being a nurse or a welder.

- Some people are drawn to work that does good for others: what is often called a vocation. Social workers, school teachers and nursery nurses might all be examples of this. There are also those individuals who work for very little or no money in charity shops and voluntary schemes.

- Some people are keen to build a career, perhaps to be promoted but also to learn a trade properly. Training for a particular vocation or studying for extra qualifications can mean that, initially, some types of work pay very little at first but have higher financial rewards later. Examples might be plumbers and lawyers.

Work can be such an important part of life, of who you are and what you do, that even people who come into a great deal of money sometimes decide to carry on working. Example 1.1 below is from a newspaper article about someone who could not give up work even though she had won the UK National Lottery. Would you give up work if you won the lottery?

Example 1.1

Julie Jeffery is showing me her home improvements. To be honest, they are nothing spectacular – two new fences, and her husband Chris laid a patio and is thinking about a vegetable patch. She lives in a modest semi in Watford where she and Chris grew up. They were both working when they won, but they were barely scraping by. Julie had worked out that she had £75 left for the next month, once the bills had been paid, and was seriously thinking of not buying a lottery ticket that week, but then changed her mind because she felt sure that if she missed a week, her numbers would come up.

She still works at the local fire station as a cook … 'We actually won on June 26 2002, and it was £1,038,970. I wanted the £38,970; I wanted someone else to take away the million …'

I ask Amanda [Julie's daughter, aged 17] … if she's got stingy parents. 'Yeah, dead stingy,' and she laughs.

Julie says it's important that the kids have a work ethic. Amanda, she says, is currently working part-time at Woolworths …

… She and Chris coped by putting it [their lottery win] into context: £1m meant 20 grand a year for the next 50 years, so there was no way they would stop working, although Chris, a kitchen-planner, has gone part-time.

…

At work, they were even more surprised that she was staying than that she had won. What does she think life would be like now if she had quit?

'I would be big as a house, probably depressed, and very bored. I certainly wouldn't be the person I am and the person I've been, because I need to work.'

(Source: Hattenstone, 2004)

1.2 Theories about motivation at work

There is no one definition of what motivation is, but it basically involves looking at the factors which cause us to behave (or not) in certain ways. Arnold et al. (1995, p. 211) suggest that is made up of three components:

1 *direction*: what a person is trying to do

2 *effort*: how hard a person is trying

3 *persistence*: how long a person continues trying.

Work takes up such a large proportion of our lives that we want to feel we are getting something from it. Ideas about what our individual needs and expectations might be will vary according to the perspective or theory that is used. Three of the most famous theories are considered below. They have been chosen because they represent three different ways of thinking about motivation; that is, *types* of people (McGregor), the *content* of motivation (Maslow) and the *process* of motivation (Vroom). There are many more theories about motivation at work, each reflecting not only the societal and business context in which it was developed but also different perspectives on people and work.

Douglas McGregor (1906–1964)

Douglas McGregor's (1960) Theory X and Theory Y is one of the most well-known models of motivation in business studies. Basically, it comprises two different perspectives on individuals at work: the kind of people they are and what managers need to do to keep them working. Theories X and Y can be thought of as two different sets of assumptions that lead managers in a business to adopt two different management styles.

Theory X managers believe that workers are motivated only by money. They are lazy, dislike work and lack ambition. They need to be controlled and coerced.

Theory Y managers believe that workers are motivated by many needs. They can take pride and responsibility in doing a good job. Management should trust workers and help them to do their best.

As with many other concepts we deal with in this course, it is all about perception. As the founder or owner of a business, for example, how you perceive what the business is for, what your role is within it and what employees do will affect business activity and the types of policies and procedures that are used.

Abraham Maslow (1908–1970)

Abraham Maslow's (1943) is the most famous of a group of theories which suggest that motivation is based on psychological need. When our needs are unmet, we experience tension that we try to put right. In other words, we behave in ways that satisfy our needs. Maslow believed that all people are motivated by the same things, but that there are different levels of need. When one set of needs in the *hierarchy* has been met, we work harder to fulfil the next level. Maslow's model is shown in Figure 1.1.

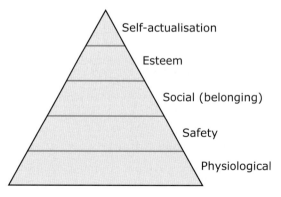

Figure 1.1 Maslow's hierarchy of needs (Source: Maslow, 1954, in Tyler, 2004, p. 262, Figure 13.3)

According to Maslow, the needs in the hierarchy have several properties:

- A need is not effective as a motivator until the 'lower level' needs are met.

- A satisfied need is not a motivator. If you are safe and well fed, you turn your attention elsewhere.

- We have an inbuilt desire to work our way up through the hierarchy of needs.

- Not meeting these needs has a negative effect on our mental health.

- The experience of *self-actualisation* (a difficult and controversial concept which Maslow argued to be the ultimate human goal, very rarely attained) stimulates the desire for more. This cannot be satisfied in the way that the other needs can.

Many businesses have used Maslow's hierarchy when establishing their HRM policies. Some simple examples of how meeting these needs might be translated into HRM policies are shown in Table 1.1.

Table 1.1 Meeting Maslow's needs through HRM policies

These needs	can be met through
Physiological	good working conditions attractive wage or salary subsidised housing free or subsidised catering
Safety	private health insurance cover attractive pension provisions safe working conditions 'no redundancy' policy
Relationships	company sports and social clubs office parties, barbeques, outings permission for informal activities encouraging open communications
Esteem	regular positive feedback prestige job titles photographs in company news sheet promotions
Self-actualisation	challenging job assignments discretion over core work activities promotion opportunities encouraging creativity

(Source: Buchanan and Huczynski, 1991, p. 61)

Maslow's idea of there being a hierarchy of needs that individuals strive to meet has proved to be both popular and influential. However, it has not been verified or 'proved' by research and has been criticised because it suggests a rather rigid structure. People may, in fact, have very different priorities at different times in their lives or stages in their careers. Individuals might move from one level of the needs hierarchy to another but have all levels of need simultaneously. Even someone close to self-actualisation will be upset if their salary is reduced!

Victor Vroom (b. 1932)

Whereas need theories like Maslow's place heavy emphasis on the content of
motivation, expectancy theory concentrates on the *process*. Expectancy
theory aims to explain how people choose which course of action to take.
Victor Vroom (1964) used the term 'subjective probability' to describe an
individual's expectation that certain behaviours would lead to a particular
outcome. This choice is conscious, he argues, and based on consideration of
the following three factors:

1 *Expectancy* If I tried, would I be able to perform the action I am
considering?

2 *Instrumentality* Would performing these actions lead to identifiable
outcomes?

3 *Valence* How much do I value these outcomes?

Expectancy theory stresses that it is not just having a reward or incentive
that is important in motivating behaviour, but rather the link between effort
and reward. Some rewards come anyway, regardless of the effort put in, and
are not likely to be effective as motivators. For example, in much of the
voluntary and public sectors, pay has traditionally been linked to the job
people do rather than to their performance in that job. Some rewards are
linked directly to effort, and they can motivate people. Other rewards are
linked to effort in a 'probabilistic' way. For a reward to affect a person's
decision to exert effort, that person must believe that the effort will increase
the likelihood of obtaining the reward.

As an equation, expectancy is:

$$F = E \times I \times V$$

Where:

F = the motivation or force to behave;

E = the perceived probability that effort will result in good performance;

I = the perceived probability that good performance will lead to a
particular outcome;

V = the perceived value that an individual has for this outcome.

In most circumstances, however, a number of different outcomes will result
from a particular behaviour. The complete equation is therefore:

$$F = \sum (E \times I \times V)$$

The sign $\sum$ is the Greek letter *sigma* which here means 'add up all the
values of the calculation in the brackets'. The force of a person's motivation
is the result of multiplying the three variables in the brackets, since if one of
these is zero then, despite the value of the others, their motivation will be
zero.

Unlike Maslow's content theory of motivation, expectancy theory is based
on individual differences and an attempt to measure the strength of
motivation. Expectancy theory assumes that people at work are motivated by
the desire to maximise the value of their 'exchange' with the business they
work for. Sometimes the costs of working hard – such as stress and less time

spent with family – will be outweighed by the expected benefits that working harder may bring, such as increased salary and promotion. In other words, people choose how hard they want to work, and feel motivated when the linkage between effort, performance and reward is clear.

Activity 1.2

Spend about **15 minutes** on this activity

Purpose: to clarify understanding of expectancy theory.

Task: complete the following questions to help you reflect on expectancy theory in the context of how hard you might be willing to work for this course and the rewards that might ensue.

1   How much will the effort you put into this course determine your performance on it? Mention other factors that you think will affect your performance.

2   What rewards will materialise if you perform well – or what costs if you perform badly? Your anticipated rewards could be those which you can see (extrinsic) and those you feel within yourself (intrinsic).

3   How much of a link is there between the value you place on these rewards and the effort you are putting into this course?

Feedback

Attempts have been made to calculate mathematical formulae that plot the link between effort, performance and reward. Your answers to the activity above may have confirmed that there are strong links between the three but that they are often very difficult to quantify. It might be worth sharing with your fellow students your answers or your thoughts about doing this activity, using the tutor group forum.

There is always a need to stop and think about theories, especially those that concern people. For example, do we as individuals really calculate the probable outcomes of particular courses of action in such a detached way as expectancy theory suggests? It could be argued that, for much of the time, calculating outcomes in this way is almost automatic and unconscious. We all have expectations about what might happen as a result of our behaviour, and what we consider desirable or undesirable will depend on our individual personalities.

Despite these potential weaknesses, expectancy theory has proved useful to business organisations because it provides an *analytical framework* to help think about both individuals' satisfaction with their jobs and possible causes of poor performance. It suggests that it might be possible to identify which feature of a person's life at work is valued by them and therefore might have an influence on their expectations and performance. If some aspects of work cause dissatisfaction, it might be possible to change these. One area of business research which looks at this is job design, which is discussed in study Session 2 of this book.

The ability of a single theory to predict and explain behaviour in these increasingly complex times is declining. The next section describes the relatively new concept of the psychological contract that has emerged as a way of addressing these issues, while providing new insights into motivation at work.

1.3 Employee expectations and the psychological contract

In order to place motivation issues in a more contemporary context we need to consider how businesses and their employees have changed. Businesses today need to be flexible and able to adapt, and to deal, for example, with international, not just national, markets. Employees, on the other hand, are much more concerned with quality of life for themselves and their families; they expect much more than previous generations from both work and their employers.

Activity 1.3

Spend about **15 minutes** on this activity

Purpose: to reflect on the changing expectations of both employees and employers in the business world.

Task: make a list of the types of expectations you might imagine employees and employers (businesses) have about work in the twenty-first century.

Feedback

You may have found this activity difficult in that you will have realised that the expectations of both employees and employers will vary according to who they are and what the business is. A young person leaving school will have different expectations of work from the person in their mid-twenties who is seeking a change of career. Expectations of employers or businesses will vary according to factors such as size, sector and values. In working through the activity you may have generated a long list which will, of course, reflect your own personality and experiences and what you might want and expect from work. Here are some of the things we thought of. For the individual: safe working conditions; job security; satisfying and challenging work; to be treated with respect; their contribution and effort recognised; to be involved in business decisions as appropriate. For the business: employees would be expected to work hard, adhere to reasonable standards of dress and behaviour, show loyalty and contribute to teamwork if appropriate. You probably had many more on your list. There is no right answer, but it is interesting to think that expectations of work and what motivates us to keep doing it are often not immediately obvious.

The psychological contract

One of the most prolific areas of research within HRM in recent years has been the concept of the ***psychological contract***. The psychological contract between employer and employee differs from a written employment contract in that it is concerned with implicit expectations, obligations and promises that both parties believe have been made with regard to what each owes and expects to receive from the other. For example, an individual may have reason to believe that they will be recognised and promoted if they work hard, even though this is not part of any formal employment contract. If this does not occur as expected, they may feel that their psychological contract has been violated, leading to dissatisfaction. A 'healthy' psychological contract is linked to outcomes such as positive employment relations, employee commitment, motivation and job satisfaction. This means that, if an individual feels that they are treated fairly and their expectations are met at work, they are more likely to feel committed to their employer and motivated to work hard for them. On the other hand, those who have a weak psychological contract with their employer will be less motivated and more likely to leave the business. Research has shown that the most significant factor associated with employees having a positive psychological contract is the existence of a larger number of fair and effective HRM practices in the business (Guest, 2001).

The psychological contract is of special interest to both students and practitioners of HRM because there is little doubt that, since the 1980s, the employment relationship has changed dramatically in most developed countries. There are many reasons for this, some of which you may already be familiar with. Increased competition brought about by *globalisation* and technological advances have obliged many businesses to restructure their operations, away from traditional hierarchies towards flatter, leaner structures. This has resulted in an increased use of teams and a greater level of responsibility for those teams and individuals. The negative side of these changes has been a decrease in job security for many people, epitomised by an increase in temporary and fixed-term employment contracts, as employers seek to maximise efficiency. Concurrently, in some European contexts, there has been a decline in the power of trade unions.

'How do you feel about letting your people work from home?'

One of the main impacts on the psychological contract in recent times is the introduction of *flexible working* for employees. Table 1.2 lists some of the new flexible forms of working that have emerged, along with changes in business practice and employee expectations. Have a look at the statistics and then complete the activity that follows.

Table 1.2 Picture of employment in the UK

% of employees involved in:	2004	1998
Homeworking	28	16
School term-time only	28	14
Flexitime	26	19
Job sharing	41	31

(Source: based on a survey of more than 3,000 workplaces in the UK, Ward and Inman, 2005, p. 8)

Activity 1.4

Spend about **20 minutes** on this activity

Purpose: to reflect on some of the potentially positive and negative aspects of flexible working.

Task: having considered the statistics in Table 1.2, reflect on what you consider to be the possible advantages and disadvantages for both employer and employee of three new ways of working: homeworking, flexitime and job sharing.

Feedback

There is now much legislation in many countries supporting people's rights for equal opportunities, parental leave and so on. As Table 1.2 shows, working at home and part-time working is not unusual. Even if you have not worked yourself or have never experienced flexi-working, it is probable that you were able to think of some advantages and disadvantages. People like working at home because it allows them to fit work around their other responsibilities, but there is a danger of feeling isolated and missing the social side of going to work which is so important for many people. The cost to the employer includes being unable to control the work being done and the potential costs of providing equipment and developing an effective information technology (IT) system which can cope efficiently with remote working. Individuals who are able to work at home or on a part-time basis may feel that it demonstrates trust and support on the part of their employer. Their motivation, and thus productivity, may well be higher.

1.4 Measuring demotivation: absenteeism

How can a business recognise when its employees are feeling *demotivated* at work? It is not always obvious when people feel unhappy with their job or with the business they work for. Demotivation is often signalled by a higher than average level of absence from work. When this happens, costs are incurred by the business. An individual's absence from work may be an indication of their need for a temporary break from work or, more seriously, a direct result of stress-induced illness. Stress has been recognised (see, for example, Cooper, 2000) as one of the highest single costs to business; it is also thought to be a significant factor in high levels of turnover (people leaving the business). Increased levels of absenteeism and turnover are often found in occupations with high levels of physical and emotional stress, such as the health care professions.

One of the most influential research studies into the factors affecting absenteeism was carried out by Steers and Rhodes (1978). It suggests that attendance at work is affected by two important variables: first, a person's motivation to work and, second, their ability to do their job. Steers and Rhodes's model is shown in Figure 1.2.

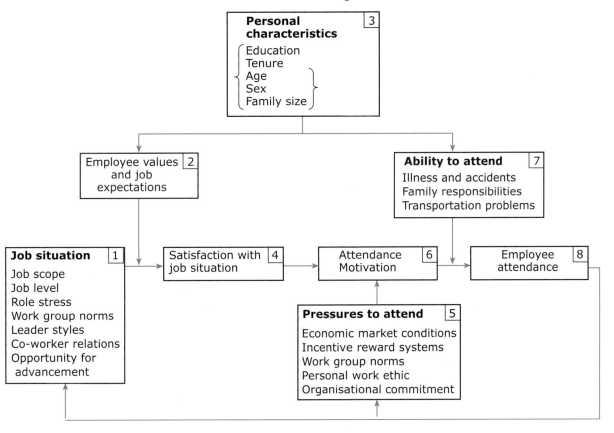

Figure 1.2 A model of employee attendance (Source: Steers and Rhodes, 1978, p. 153, Figure 12.1)

The authors suggest that the dimension of 'ability to attend' (box 7 in Figure 1.2) is an important addition to theories about absenteeism as many studies fail to take into account the case of *involuntary* absenteeism. This occurs when an individual may want to attend work, and probably has a low absence record, but attendance is not possible and there is no choice available.

Activity 1.5

Spend about **20 minutes** on this activity

Purpose: to reinforce understanding of Steers and Rhodes's theory of absenteeism by placing it in today's business context.

Task: look again at Steers and Rhodes's model in Figure 1.2. Think about, and make some notes on, how aspects of the twenty-first century business environment might make a difference to motivation and absenteeism at work today compared with motivation and absenteeism in the 1970s when the model was developed.

Feedback

While Steers and Rhodes's model is still influential, today's work and business environments and societal attitudes are different from those of the 1970s. Some factors in Figure 1.2 may have changed or be more or less important. For example, today's uncertain job market and fear of recession could affect absence levels as employees face uncertainty about the security of their jobs and suffer from stress as a result of this. On the other hand, employees may have higher expectations of work and expect more support from employers in terms of flexible working practices.

It may not seem unreasonable that many businesses monitor levels of employee absence. However, there must always be the danger that, in trying to reduce overall absence figures, an atmosphere of hostility and resentment may result from employees in the business. A feeling of being closely monitored at work may well result in the demotivation that you are trying to avoid. Read Example 1.2 about the supermarket chain, Tesco, and reflect on how you might feel as an employee subjected to their 'attendance management procedures'.

Example 1.2

The country's largest private sector employer, Tesco, has concluded that there are many attitudinal factors in taking sick leave. 'If you don't think you are likely to be missed, you are more likely to take time off,' says Keith Luxon, human resources policy manager. A year ago, Tesco's absenteeism rate was 5.8 per cent. Now it is down by a fifth to 4.6 per cent.

This follows the implementation of new 'attendance management procedures'. As a result, some of the supermarket chain's 175,000 workers have been dismissed because of the time they have taken off sick. Some may think this is a harsh approach, but Tesco is happy to talk about its reasons.

'We wanted more openness and honesty about absence,' says Luxon. 'We are operating in an incredibly tight market which is forcing us to control costs wherever we can. Absenteeism was costing us between [£]30 million and [£]40 m a year, and it was impacting on customer service. If you operate with 5.8 per cent of your staff away, you have fewer tills open and fewer goods on the shelf.'

Every Tesco employee who takes sick leave of any duration has to have a 'return to work' interview with one of the store managers. In a substantial number of cases, it has emerged that the person was off for domestic or family reasons – looking after a sick child, for example. If this is the case, the employee is given various options about how they want to treat that time: it could be taken as holiday, as unpaid leave, or set off against overtime, but they will not get it for free.

People who have two periods of sickness within 24 weeks are then drawn into the 'attendance management' process, where their attendance is monitored. If they then have a third absence, or if their total time off sick goes above 5 per cent, they are interviewed again and banned from doing overtime for six weeks.

In the interview, they will be asked more about their time off – whether there are common patterns to the different periods of illness. Occupational health services will be made available if a pattern is established – if, for example, they are suffering from repeated back trouble or if they want to space their shifts out differently. If over the next 12 weeks their sickness record does not improve, they get another interview and probably a verbal warning. They will be told: 'We can't run a business effectively on this level of absence.'

If within the next eight weeks there is no improvement in absenteeism levels, they could get a final written warning, and then it is possible that they could be sacked.

Tesco says it has tried to be fair and open with staff. An employee will not have to go through this process if there is a clear medical problem.

(Source: MacErlean, 2000, p. 14)

1.5 Conclusion

To conclude this study session on why people go to work we should recognise that many theories about motivation at work are built on assumptions that we might question in today's context. For example, they often assume job security and a relatively standardised, non-diverse workforce. In the next study session we consider the related concept of job satisfaction and some theories of job design.

1.6 Learning outcomes

By the end of this study session on why people go to work you should be able to:

- explain some of the factors that motivate people to want to work for a business;
- outline the main ideas underpinning three famous theories of motivation;
- discuss the importance of the psychological contract;
- describe some of the advantages and disadvantages of absence management programmes.

You will have developed your learning by:

- being introduced to the significant increases in new, flexible forms of working;
- applying expectancy theory to your own motivations as a student on this course.

Session 2 Designing satisfying work

Why are we studying 'designing satisfying work'? The way in which work is organised and designed within a business impacts on both the effectiveness of the business and the experiences of the individual and work group within it.

The **aims and objectives** of Session 2 are to:

- describe the factors that can affect job satisfaction;
- evaluate the job characteristics model and its implications for job redesign;
- provide an introduction to scientific management (or Taylorism);
- discuss the potential benefits and problems of the introduction of semi-autonomous teams and relate this to a practical business situation.

2.1 Enthusiasm for work

A business can thrive only if the people who work for it are committed to its success. Getting individuals enthused about going to work and making sure their skills and abilities are being utilised effectively is one of the key components of HRM. Given that everyone is different and, as we saw in the previous study session, we are all motivated by different things at different times, how is it possible to ensure that people feel satisfied with their jobs? In this study session we consider different ways of designing work within a business in an attempt to capture people's interest and productivity. Again, we must remind ourselves of the difficulties of doing this. Different ways of working will be preferred by different individuals and the work in each business will be different, depending on the circumstances and project. *Intrinsic motivation* (that is, that within us) is hard to manage and even understand. With this (perhaps annoying!) caveat in mind, we turn first to the rather complex, yet extremely influential, job characteristics model (JCM) developed by Hackman and Oldham (1980). This offers a framework for analysing, first, the key characteristics of a job and, second, the key responses to that job by the individuals doing it.

2.2 The job characteristics model

Hackman and Oldham's (1980) work on the job characteristics model inspired much research into developing a framework for analysing the content of jobs. It looks at the relationship between core job characteristics, employees' psychological states and key outcomes. The model provides a language for talking about the design of jobs within businesses and highlights the complexity of the principles involved. Hackman and Oldham's model is shown in Figure 2.1.

The different components of Hackman and Oldham's model are detailed below.

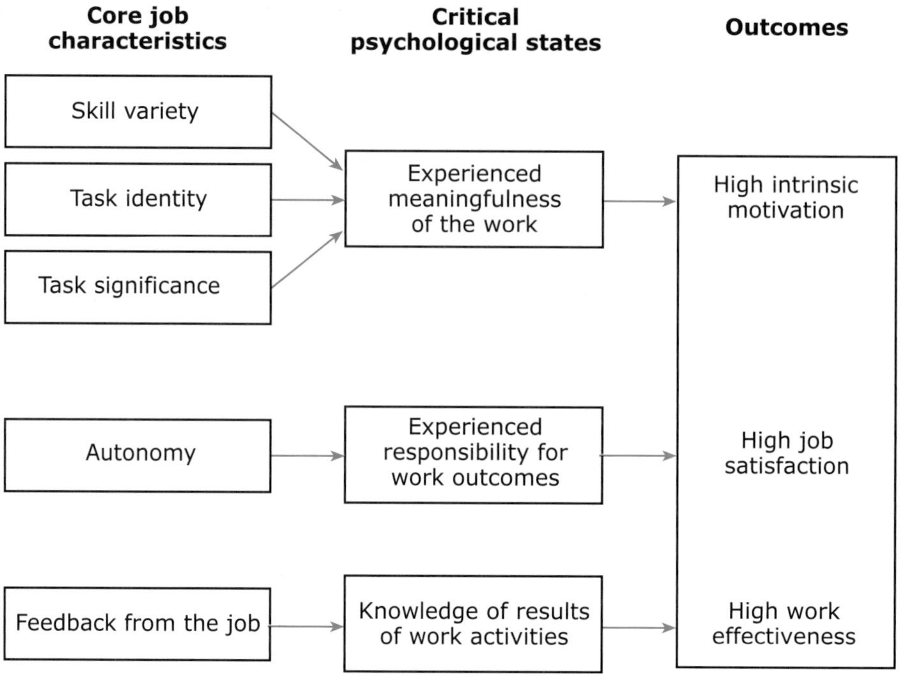

Figure 2.1 Hackman and Oldham's job characteristics model (Source: Arnold et al., 1995, p. 395, Figure 19.1)

Skill variety

Skill variety is defined as the extent to which a job includes a variety of activities and therefore requires the employee to use a number of different skills and talents. If individuals feel that anyone else could do the work and to as high a standard, they are unlikely to feel any sense of achievement from doing the job. Equally, if doing the job does not utilise their abilities and skills it is unlikely that they will be learning very much. It may not necessarily be the case that the job offers a lack of skill variety; it may just be that the person is not aware of the skills that are required. On the other hand, jobs that include too much variety are likely to feel fragmented. Employees may find that there are too many different demands on their time and they cannot develop the skills they need to do the job well. It is worth noting that much of the work on job design emerged within an industrial context and, not surprisingly, addressed issues of variety and repetition.

Task identity

Task identity is about doing a job from beginning to end. It is the extent to which the job requires completion of a whole and identifiable piece of work. It evaluates the degree to which the individual feels involved with the outcomes of their work. In many instances, adding related tasks to a job can increase task identity.

Task significance

Task significance is defined as the degree to which the job is perceived by the employee to have an impact on the lives or work of other people, whether within the business or in the external environment. Some jobs, such as health care and education, have a more obvious impact than others, but this is about employees' perceptions. In short, if employees can see how their job and contribution fit into the overall achievement of the objectives of the business, they are likely to feel more motivated than if they cannot. On this basis, effective communication systems within the business can have a positive effect on task significance.

Autonomy

Autonomy is about the extent to which the job allows the employee to exercise choice in their work. An example of this might be the opportunity to schedule or prioritise work that would give the individual a sense of responsibility for getting the job done.

Feedback from the job

This is the extent to which the job itself – as opposed to other people – provides information about how the job holder is performing. This can take the form of, for instance, seeing that an initiative or change introduced to the job is effective.

In Hackman and Oldham's model, these core job characteristics are said to produce 'critical psychological states'. These are:

- experienced meaningfulness of the work – thought to be influenced by skill variety, task identity and task significance;
- experienced responsibility for outcomes of the work – thought to be influenced by the degree of autonomy;
- knowledge of the actual results of work – affected by feedback from the job.

These in turn are believed to influence motivation, satisfaction and work performance.

Critics of the JCM (for example, Roberts and Glick, 1981) have argued that very few evaluations of the JCM have involved attempts to actually redesign jobs and to see whether the effects of job redesign have been maintained over a long period. However, the JCM has produced a huge amount of research, especially in the USA (see, for example, Maccoby, 1988). The JCM offers a very practical model which suggests that by introducing certain working practices – improving feedback, reviewing responsibilities, combining tasks, forming work groups – the motivating potential of jobs can be increased.

2.3 Job satisfaction

It is not easy to understand the nature of job satisfaction because there are so many factors that could affect a person's perception of their job at any particular time. Job satisfaction is a *feeling* about working and about the job. The following activity may help you to identify your own feelings about work.

Activity 2.1

Spend about **10 minutes** on this activity

Purpose: to apply your learning about motivation, job satisfaction and potentially motivating aspects of a job to a personal situation or experience.

Task: think about the following two questions:

1   What do you think motivates you?

2   What is important to you in a job and why?

Feedback

The cause of (dis)satisfaction for an individual at work may be the result of one or many factors. Moreover, it is likely that our satisfaction within work is both implicit (inside ourselves and difficult to articulate) and relative to our circumstances at any particular time; it is also likely to be affected by our previous jobs. We are likely to enjoy some aspects of our work but not others. There is no one theory that can explain job satisfaction, but there are some models and frameworks that can help us think about it. This is difficult for those individuals (managers and HRM people) who are responsible for both the productivity and the psychological well-being of people within a business. Some ideas about the kinds of factors which could affect motivation are listed below.

The types of factors that could impact on motivation at work are:

- *individual*: such as age, education, ability and personality;
- *social*: work relationships and the opportunity to interact with people at work, either formally or informally;
- *cultural*: underlying beliefs, attitudes and values;
- *organisational*: the nature and size of the business, the types of management and supervisory styles, the working conditions, the type of technology that is used, business policies and procedures;
- *environmental*: including economic, social, technical and governmental influences.

Many tests are available to measure individual motivations, skills and preferences. These are often called **psychometric tests** and they are used by the HRM department within a business to help with recruitment or succession planning. There are arguments for and against the usefulness of such tests, but they continue to be commonly used in, for instance, assessing people's suitability against job criteria. We found several tests for measuring job satisfaction, through a quick online search. Perhaps you would like to search for and try one of these tests now. You might learn something new about yourself!

In the next section we move from the level of the individual to that of the business with regard to job satisfaction, and look at two different approaches to job (re)design.

2.4 Job design

Job design is about how work might be organised or reorganised to meet the social needs of individuals and the operational needs of a business. Any job within a business may change as a result of either internal or external influences. Some examples of such influences are:

- a merger;
- a drop in demand for a particular type of product;
- the implementation of an equal opportunities policy;
- a new trade union agreement;
- jobs becoming too large or small as, for instance, technology develops or work teams begin to share tasks.

Both scenarios in the last bullet point have an important effect on the individual doing the job. A large job may become fragmented and overwhelming, causing stress and lowering motivation. If the job becomes too small, it may become repetitive or not challenging enough to offer any sense of achievement or opportunities for learning. In this context, people's jobs need reviewing constantly.

From an HRM point of view, some appropriate time for reviewing jobs might be at:

- Recruitment: when it is always good practice to draw up a job description before a job is advertised and to think carefully about what is involved. This is an ideal opportunity to review the content of the job and redesign it if necessary.
- An annual performance appraisal (discussed in study Session 4 of this book), which gives employees an opportunity to review their jobs with their line manager(s) and/or colleagues.
- Times of major change; for example, the introduction of new technology or restructuring.

Ideally, job reviews should be ongoing within the business.

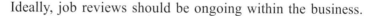

In the next two sections we compare two different approaches to job design: *scientific management* and the *socio-technical approach*.

Although developed at the start of the twentieth century, scientific management (Taylor, 1911) is still influential in business today. The worldwide fast-food chain McDonald's, for example, is scientific management in action: each employee gets another star on their badge to denote that they have become proficient in each component of the job. Let us look in more detail at the ideas and the context behind Taylor's model of job design.

'Lost my job. But I'm pretty sure it's around here somewhere.'

2.5 Taylorism

The idea that we can consciously design jobs and break them down into quantifiable components has a long history in business studies. An early example was when Frederick Taylor (1911) carefully studied the components of manufacturing jobs and calculated the most efficient ways of carrying them out. Taylor's writings continue to be influential; many businesses and jobs are still structured along the scientific management objectives of:

- *efficiency*: achieved by increasing the output per worker and reducing deliberate 'under working' by employees;
- *standardisation*: of job performance, achieved by dividing up work tasks into small and clearly specified sub-tasks;
- *discipline*: achieved by establishing hierarchical authority. One key principle of discipline was a clear division between the responsibilities and tasks of workers and managers.

Taylor's scientific management is often criticised today as being rather naive, but it is important to recognise the business environment in which his research was conducted. Business in the USA was undergoing a major industrial reorganisation in the early twentieth century.

Huge businesses such as Ford and General Motors were being created. Employees were coming from the agricultural regions of America or were immigrants from Europe seeking new lives. Directing the efforts of this huge workforce with no experience of factory work, and with perhaps a limited understanding of the English language, required a simple, clear and efficient way of organising the work. Taylor was not an academic but a practical businessman with real problems to solve. His writings represent some of the first attempts to systematically analyse work and business. Later approaches to the design of jobs argue that Taylorism represents a rather limited view of working. His idea that there was 'one best way' and that this approach would work in any business may seem naive now, but it revolutionised business thinking.

In the next section we look at a rather different approach to job design.

2.6 The socio-technical approach

Researchers at the Tavistock Institute in the UK (Trist and Bamforth, 1951) pioneered the socio-technical approach in the mid-twentieth century. They developed the idea of a business being the amalgamation of two interrelated systems: the social and the technological. Their work (in Indian textile mills and English coal mines) was based on the idea that businesses should be thought of as ever-changing and very complex systems. In terms of job design, then, seeking a technically perfect or socially perfect way is impossible. The aim should be to meet both types of need adequately.

Charlie Chaplin in the film *Modern Times*

The principles of the socio-technical approach to job design are:

- The design of one part of the system should not dictate the design of the other part.
- Job redesign should not take place in a way that is totally removed from wider factors such as culture and group identity. Changing one part of the system has implications for the other part.

- Redesign should involve employees. It should evolve in an organic way, based on recognition of the social and technological needs of the system. It should not be based on sets of general principles or techniques.

The socio-technical approach led to the development of a new way of looking at job design. The basis is that the planning of job design is part of a broader discussion about the need to balance employee input and technical parameters throughout decision-making processes. In short, it is an attempt to bring the people element back into the planning of work. Research into this area, however, tells us that businesses often find problems with the 'people' side of this type of job design.

The socio-technical approach is also a stimulating way of looking at businesses. It has had a considerable impact in terms of working practices, illustrated, for example, by the introduction of semi-autonomous work groups in many businesses. Semi-autonomous work groups are a specific type of work group in that they are self-regulating to some degree.

The problems of introducing the socio-technical approach into business are:

- *Group dynamics and interpersonal conflict.* While groups have to contain the right number of people with the right skills to do the job, there is an important interpersonal aspect to working in small groups. This can have an impact on at least two levels. First, groups can become so cohesive that adding new members becomes problematic. Second, differences in status and pay within small groups can lead to conflict.

- *The organisational context.* Factors such as pay and the structure of rewards must be appropriate. Individuals need enough information to complete tasks effectively and there has to be discrimination between **performance targets** that are challenging and those which constrain behaviour.

- *Management commitment.* Perhaps the most important factor is the degree to which there is genuine commitment to the idea of semi-autonomous working from the immediate managers and supervisors of groups of workers. Management practice has to move in the direction of increasing real autonomy and this raises the question of power and the extent to which autonomy undermines managerial power and authority. By definition, autonomy implies 'free from direct management'. It is quite possible for two parties – with their own values and perceptions – to view events quite differently.

- *Communication.* While effective communication is often cited as an advantage of the socio-technical approach, research has shown that this is not always the case. Gratton et al. (1999), for example, found that in the organisations they studied, no more than 20 per cent of employees believed that members of senior management were well informed about those aspects of working life that were important to the people at lower levels in the business.

- *The impact on people in supervisory roles* Semi-autonomous work groups by definition need less control and direction. This may present a difficulty for supervisors who have to appreciate that their role has changed. They may be aware of a loss in perceived power and status, and need help to cope with their new role.

Example 2.1 below illustrates an instance of job redesign based around semi-autonomous group working in a major UK manufacturing business.

Example 2.1

In 1992, a major UK company which manufactures high-precision components for the airline industry introduced a 'manufacturing systems engineering approach' into one of its sites. One of the main features of this approach was the introduction of autonomous 'cells' where multi-skilled, flexible, semi-autonomous teams were responsible for the production of a particular product. **Cellular organisation**, combined with just-in-time* manufacturing technology, helped to highlight bottlenecks in the production process and emphasised any factors which interfered with capacity and efficiency. Cell or team members were given control over work flow scheduling and work allocation. The intention was to encourage a change in management style to a more open, communicative and participative approach.

Over the first twelve months, results were impressive. They included:

- a capacity increase of 30 per cent;
- a reduction in manufacturing costs of 30–40 per cent;
- a response time down from 8–12 weeks to two weeks.

A questionnaire to members of the new teams also demonstrated very positive results, with high scores on job variety and interest. Respondents also appreciated the greater autonomy with regard to problem solving and the reduced level of supervision.

(***Just-in-time** refers to a philosophy developed in Japan where parts arrive from suppliers just in time to be placed in the manufacturing process. The emphasis is on enhanced speed and reduced costs.)

(Source: based on Buchanan and Preston, 1992, pp. 58–60, 62–4)

Example 2.1 above demonstrates some of the dramatic benefits gained over the first twelve months by this particular business following the introduction of semi-autonomous team working. However, there were several people issues that accompanied these results. First, supervisors at the manufacturing plant had traditionally been identified by a different coloured overall. This 'symbol' of their higher status was removed, as was most of their discretion over the decisions made: this had passed to the teams. This may seem a trivial example, but it is likely that these individuals had worked hard and for many years to gain their promotions to supervisory level. Second, employees on the shop floor were enjoying their new responsibility but, at the time of the research twelve months on, remained cynical about management motives for introducing the new way of working. One of the conclusions reached by the research was that, in this instance, it appeared that there had been insufficient input from the HRM department, resulting in greater consideration of the technical aspects than of the people (socio) aspects. This was precisely the kind of situation that Bamforth and Trist had challenged in developing their socio-technical approach some forty or more years earlier. Despite these potential problems, however, semi-autonomous working has worked well in many businesses: companies such as Fiat, Volvo, ICI and Philips have famously adopted these or very similar techniques. Improvements have ranged from increased productivity, reduction of unplanned stoppages, improved product quality and reduced absenteeism.

I was one of the two researchers involved in the business research project described in Example 2.1, in which we were asked to do an evaluation of the job redesign initiative by one of the managers on an MBA course. As an aside, when we presented our results to the production director of the business, it was clear that he did not fully understand the extent of our evaluation; that is, talking to the employees themselves. Furious, he asked us to 'stop stirring up trouble' and to leave the site. This is an aspect of business research/consultancy which is not often discussed and is worth exploring further.

Activity 2.2

Spend about **30 minutes** on this activity

Purpose: to reflect on the difficulties of carrying out research in a business.

Task: reread Example 2.1 above, describing the research project where the researchers were asked to leave the business research site before the project was finished. Can you think of any other problems that you might encounter as a student doing research within a business? What would be the main issues, do you think, under each of the following headings:

1 choosing a business to study;

2 negotiating access into the business;

3 talking to or interviewing employees and/or managers;

4 providing the business with feedback on your study.

Make some notes on your responses.

Feedback

Conducting research and developing theories about how businesses operate is a challenging proposition. Every business is different on a number of dimensions; it is also made up of different groups of individuals and, as we have tried to emphasise in this book, the subjective, or people, part of a business cannot be conveniently ignored. We thought of the following issues concerned with the four stages listed above; you may have others.

1   Choosing which business to study is always an issue and would need sound justification in terms of the research study proposal. This clearly depends on the issues you want to explore. We chose a manufacturing business because we were looking at semi-autonomous teams. If you were interested in tele-working you might choose a call centre. If you were interested in autonomous working, you may choose a research and development environment. You may well want to focus on one type of business or business sector in your research.

2   Businesses tend to be quite wary of researchers being on their premises. It could involve extra work or distraction for their employees, or they may be afraid that business procedures and sales results, for example, could be leaked to their competitors. It is important for a business researcher to contact the appropriate person; that is, someone who can make a decision about access. It is also crucial that everyone involved, including senior management, is very clear about who the researcher is and what the aims of the study are.

3   Planning appropriate questions and actually getting employees to talk to you about the issues that interest you can be problematic. Apart from taking up their time, there may be 'hidden agendas' in terms of the business or political issues between different groups of employees that will influence their responses.

4   It is essential that the researcher provides some written feedback to the business at the end of the study. Good manners and professional practice demand this. Feedback also provides reassurance about the way in which the collected information will be used and can help to keep the lines of communication open for further stages of the study.

Activity 2.2 above demonstrates the complexity of finding out more about businesses in a context that is constantly changing and is affected by many STEEP (social, technological, economic, environmental and political) factors. You might like to think about your next visit to a business (be it a hairdresser, supermarket, hospital, etc.) from the perspective of a business researcher.

2.7 Conclusion

In this study session about designing satisfying work, we have seen how much research has grown up around the question of how to capture people's motivation and interest in their work, thereby (theoretically at least) increasing productivity and effectiveness within a business. Breaking jobs down into identifiable components in the way of the JCM and scientific management models may seem inappropriate, taking insufficient account of the social aspect of working in a business. However, the JCM does offer an opportunity to think more carefully about what a job entails and how it can be made more interesting. We also looked at the socio-technical approach to job design which highlights the necessity to give equal importance to the social aspects of work. We then considered a real-life example of the benefits and drawbacks of semi-autonomous team working and explored some issues around doing research on the people side of business. In the next study session we begin to explore some of the main activities of the HRM function within a business.

2.8 Learning outcomes

By the end of this study session on designing satisfying work you should be able to:

- explain the job characteristics model and its usefulness in job (re)design;
- outline some of the triggers for a review of jobs within a business;
- describe the approach and objectives of scientific management;
- present the advantages and disadvantages of a socio-technical approach to job (re)design.

You will have developed your learning by:

- applying the theory of the socio-technical approach to a real business situation;
- reflecting on the issues involved in carrying out research in business generally.

Session 3 Finding people and helping them fit in

Why are we studying 'finding people and helping them fit'? Attracting people to apply to work for a business and being able to select the right mix of skills and personalities is crucial to the continuation of any business. Once recruited, there is then the issue of helping new employees to find their place and understand what is required of them. This entry stage of HRM is an extremely important one.

The **aims and objectives** of Session 3 are to:

- describe the recruitment process as a two-way activity;
- highlight the dangers of stereotyping and discrimination in the recruitment process;
- outline the main methods of selecting employees;
- explain the processes of, and the differences between, induction and socialisation.

3.1 First impressions

We have established that businesses cannot run unless there are people there to run them. Attracting the right individuals with the right skills to work for a business is a key element of its success. This entry point into the business and the impressions formed by both the employer and employee at this stage are significant. There are many recruitment and selection methods available to help to structure this process, but there will always be an emotive element: people choosing people with whom they want to work. Part of recruitment is anticipating the potential of an individual to develop and learn new skills and be able to adapt to the job and the business. 'Past performance predicts future performance' is an old adage, but how can we be sure this is the case? As we have seen in earlier study sessions of this book, it is essential that people are motivated to work. Making them aware of what the job is, what is expected and the overall values of the business are important from the start. Whatever the job the person is doing, a key question is whether they develop any kind of commitment to the business and what it is trying to achieve. Is it right to expect this? And what sort of training and development activities can be used to develop those specific skills and overall commitment seen as critical to business success? It is to these questions that we now turn.

3.2 Recruitment

Towards the end of the 1980s, the recruitment and selection of employees was seen as the key issue for businesses in the developed world. As businesses and the jobs within them changed, the types of skills needed were in short supply. Added to this was the so-called 'demographic time bomb' where the number of young people who were going to be available to enter work was declining significantly. The position of power, it was predicted, was shifting away from employers to those employees with the right skills to offer, and business would require a radical response. The deep recession at the end of the 1980s meant that this never really happened. However, as we have seen in previous study sessions of this book, the expectations of today's employees are significantly different from what they were even ten or fifteen years ago. The costs of recruitment for a business are significant and, if appointees don't 'fit' (and then leave) the business, profitability is further affected.

Much of the business literature about recruitment and selection is about the different methods that can be used by HRM and line managers to try to lessen the subjectivity of the process. It is said, for example, that people make up their minds about an interviewee within the first three minutes of an interview.

In this study session we need to learn something about what these different methods are, but we also need to be aware that, conducted properly, recruitment is a two-way process. It may not feel like this when we are applying for jobs, but the recruitment process should be as much about the applicant finding out whether the business is right for them as about whether they are deemed acceptable by the business.

Activity 3.1

Spend about **10 minutes** on this activity

Purpose: to reflect on the idea of recruitment being a two-way process.

Task: take a few minutes to reflect on the following two questions:

1 How realistic do you think it is to suggest that there are some situations where the interviewee has more 'power' than the employer?

2 Can you think of any situations where this might be the case?

Feedback

In certain situations the power may lie with the applicant; for example, in a sector or country where the demand for employees is high but supply is low. In the new city of Milton Keynes in the UK, for example, the home of The Open University, the unemployment rate is extremely low compared with the national average. New businesses moving into the city face massive competition from other companies searching for high-calibre staff.

Example 3.1 provides a further illustration of a business having to adjust HRM policy to accommodate a declining supply of employees.

Example 3.1

Lufthansa is one of the top airlines in the world, serving 47 million customers in 2000. However, the continuing success of the company, overall economic growth and a declining birth-rate in Germany resulted recently in a lack of suitable applicants for certain jobs within the company. Recognising that today's younger generation tend to prioritise the search for challenging jobs over the need for life long employment, Lufthansa changed its recruitment strategies. Rather than placing advertisements in national newspapers, for example, they switched to targeted recruitment using specialist magazines and radio programmes. The use of the Internet was also introduced where information about the organisation was made available directly to applicants and also allowed them to apply on-line. In addition to new recruitment strategies, Lufthansa has worked hard to change its HR policy to enhance the retention of quality staff. The development of the payment and benefits systems included the introduction of an employee share ownership programme and more opportunities to work flexibly. In 2000, 45% of Lufthansa employees had contracted into the employee share scheme and 21% of employees were on part time contracts.

(Source unknown)

Recruitment is often underrated as a communications function within a business. Any process of recruitment, whether it be an advertisement or a 'drop-in' day for interested candidates, is saying something to the outside world about how the business presents itself. Advertisements and general coverage in the media lead us all to have assumptions and expectations about what particular businesses would be like to work for. In opting to apply for a job we are bound to have ideas about what we might expect to find there. Recruitment and selection is a two-way process with information from both the applicant and the employer as to what each has to offer. This point is highlighted in the simple illustration in Example 3.2.

Example 3.2

Rita was really pleased to have been asked to an interview for the job of partner liaison manager for a national charity. She spent a lot of time preparing for the interview, finding out more about this and other charities in her local library and on the internet. It also took her a long time to put together all the required documentation, such as original copies of all qualification certificates and three additional references.

On the day of the interview, Rita arrived early but was not asked into the interview room until 30 minutes after her allotted time. The first thing she was asked to do by a member of the panel was 'describe your major weaknesses and what you have done to overcome them'. This completely surprised Rita and she struggled to respond. It was not a good start. A second member of the panel quizzed her closely about her fluency in other languages but was sharply reminded by his colleague that it was not that job they were interviewing for. The third member of the panel explained that he was the current line manager for this role but that he would be retiring before the person they appointed would start the job. The fourth member of the panel did ask some relevant questions, but all the time that Rita was responding to his questions, he was looking through a pile of papers on the desk in front of him. The panel did not ask to see Rita's portfolio of documents and could not say when she or the other applicants would know of their decision.

Rita received a letter a week later offering her the job; she decided not to accept.

You might like to think about whether you agree with her decision or not, and why.

Stereotyping

Many people are deterred from entering certain professions because of general, stereotypical images which exist in their society or culture. In a study of the attractiveness of the National Health Service in the UK as an employer (Arnold et al., 2003), for example, it was found that many men still felt that nursing was an unattractive occupation. Apart from the traditional stereotyping of nursing as a female occupation, a strong image was of 'messy', distressing and sometimes intimate work with patients. It was also perceived to be highly stressful and underpaid. On the other hand, many men said that they would consider a career in physiotherapy. This was because the predominant image was of working with sports teams, although this is in fact a very minor part of what physiotherapists do. In their efforts to recruit staff, the challenge for the NHS as a prospective employer was how to address these established, public understandings of what a career in health care would involve.

We can explore subconscious stereotyping by completing the following activity.

Activity 3.2

Spend about **10 minutes** on this activity

Purpose: to explore stereotyping in recruitment and selection procedures.

Task: make a list of about five jobs you can think of. Try not to use obvious ones or generic ones such as 'manager', but something more specific such as milkman or policewoman. For each of your chosen jobs jot down some ideas about the characteristics that might be associated with them. Don't take too much time to think – just jot down ideas as they come to you.

Feedback

We have compiled lists for three different jobs in the table below; you may not agree with the stereotyping evident in the suggested characteristics!

Job	Age	Gender	Politics	Hobbies	Car
Social worker	27– 43	Either	Liberal or Green	Camping, rambling	Old Volvo
Senior civil servant	48– 65	Male	Conservative	Opera	Jaguar
Supermarket checkout operative	25– 40	Female	Socialist	Bingo	Ford

Stereotyping can be a real problem for some businesses as they may experience recruitment difficulties because people might not want to be associated with them. Take a look at Example 3.3 below about the Scout Association.

Example 3.3

A shortage of adult volunteers willing to lead youngsters is forcing Scout groups to address their traditional methods of recruitment … Caroline O'Hagan shatters a few stereotypes about your average Scout leader. A 25-year-old senior account manager at a public relations firm in south-west London, O'Hagan – known as 'CJ' – is also assistant Scout leader for the 13th Twickenham group, which takes care of her Thursday evenings and a bit more besides.

For her, Scouting has meant travelling the world. It has also led to fulfilling friendships and a raft of transferable skills from leadership to learning how to budget. She is aware, however, that Scout leaders have something of an image problem.

'The reality and people's perception are totally out of step with one another,' O'Hagan says. 'Male adults can find it hard coming out to friends about what they do in their spare time. I think it is a problem with society in general if people think there must be something wrong if you want to work with young people.'

Her frustration is understandable. As many as 26,000 girls and boys in Britain are currently waiting for a place at their local Cub or Scout group. Over at Girlguiding UK, the problem is even worse, with 50,000 hopefuls on Brownie or Guide waiting lists. St John Ambulance, another organisation for uniformed youngsters, tells a similar story of group closures despite lists of eager would-be joiners.

The underlying problem is an acute shortage of adult volunteers willing to lead children and young people. Yet 2005 has been designated the Year of the Volunteer, supported by the Home Office, and volunteering has never been so high on the agenda. According to CSV (Community Service Volunteers) – which works with 129,000 volunteers – youth groups need to rethink their traditional approach to recruitment, recognising that people may these days be looking for some kind of personal growth through volunteering.

'People will get involved if you give them something they want to do,' argues CSV spokesman Martin Walford. 'It has to be a meaningful project which makes a difference. Most volunteers want to do something that is a challenge and innovative. They want to learn from it and get as much as they give. The days when volunteers were happy to stuff envelopes have gone.'

Some of the larger youth organisations have already started to adjust, looking to attract people who may work long hours and jealously guard their leisure time. The message is that working with children and young people can be an exciting, even career-enhancing way of spending your spare time – however limited that may be. Many organisations are adopting the jargon of the modern workplace, so that leaders are now offered job-sharing, flexible working and training via e-learning.

(Source: Coombes, 2005)

3.3 Selection

Finding the right people to work for the business involves establishing a good understanding of the types of jobs that exist and the particular skills and attributes that are involved. It is usually the responsibility of the HRM function or representative to do what is called a job analysis from which a detailed description of a job can be produced. The types of questions that might be asked about the job would be:

- What is the job holder responsible for? – Budgets? The work of others? Resources?

- What sorts of working relationships are involved? – With colleagues, customers, other departments or businesses, for example?

- What are the job requirements? – Types of skills and experience? Required standard of performance? Physical attributes?

- What are the working conditions? – The physical environment, the pay, the group, etc.?

These types of questions would be asked of both the person still in the role and their line manager in order to establish whether any changes are imminent. Consideration might also be given to whether the vacant job needs to be filled at all. Reallocation of work, internal promotion or temporary transfer could be used to cover the tasks associated with the vacancy within the business.

The job description

From the job analysis a job description is written that will state what the job holder is responsible for and what they are required to do. An accurate job description has various uses outside the recruitment process: for example, it can be used to review staff performance in appraisals or to assess training needs when someone new starts with the business. Within the recruitment process, the job description leads on to the next stage of specifying the type of person the business is looking for to fill the vacancy. This is called the person specification.

The person specification

It is important for the business to be as precise as possible about the skills, knowledge, qualifications and attributes that are required for the job, and about the experience and personal characteristics that are needed. It is good practice to specify what is essential or the minimum required to perform the job, as well as what is desirable. To decide on the qualities required for the person specification, key features are identified from the job description. The context of the job and the wider business requirements should also be considered.

Activity 3.3

Spend about **20 minutes** on this activity

Purpose: to clarify your understanding of job descriptions and person specifications.

Task: choose a particular job with which you are familiar or might be interested in applying for. If stuck, you could use one of the examples in Activity 3.2 in which we looked at the stereotyping effects of recruitment. For your chosen job, make notes to the best of your ability for the points listed below:

1 physical attributes needed for the job

2 mental attributes

3 education and qualifications

4 experience, training and skills

5 personality

6 special circumstances.

Feedback

There are no right answers to this activity, but it should have demonstrated how difficult it is when one starts to think in detail about the requirements for a particular job. Check back over what you have written, bearing the following points in mind:

- Have you thought about the qualities needed to cope with the difficult parts of the job?
- Have you considered any particular qualities that would be required to fit the culture of the business?
- How carefully have you thought through the education/training needed for the work? Remember that qualifications are only one way of knowing what people have to offer. Skills and experience gained in a whole variety of contexts – for example, parenting, voluntary work, leisure interests – can sometimes be just as relevant.
- Have you included any rigid requirements based on age, physical ability and length of paid work experience which may be questionable on equal opportunities grounds and constitute 'indirect discrimination' (specifying a criterion that would effectively debar someone because of their ethnicity, gender, age, disability or sexual orientation, for instance)?
- It is a good idea to say which qualities and attributes you consider to be essential and which desirable. Remember, if something is 'essential' you should be able to justify it.
- Is the specification credible? Do such people exist? Are they likely to apply for the salary offered? What are the options if the answers to these questions are 'no'?

Selection methods

The main methods of selecting potential employees for a business are:

- *Interviews* The aim of the selection interview is to determine whether the candidate is interested in the job and competent to do it. It is also used to explain the work of both the business and the job and to establish expectations on both sides. In terms of it being a two-way process as discussed earlier, it is also a chance for the applicant to assess whether they want the job being offered. Interviews are often criticised as being too subjective; individual biases and prejudice get in the way of an objective assessment of an individual's abilities. We explored the dangers of stereotyping in section 3.2 of study Session 3. It can be argued, however, that most people expect to be interviewed. This may contribute to the fact that it is by far the most common type of selection method.
- *Tests* There are various types of tests and ways in which they might be used as part of the selection process. Tests can be used to measure aptitude, such as competence in literacy or numeracy, or personality (often called psychometric tests, which we looked at briefly in section 2.3 of study Session 2). Tests and their results are likely to form a part rather than the whole of a selection process as they provide ***quantitative*** but not ***qualitative*** information about an individual. (The difference between

quantitative and qualitative, in the context of setting standards, is explained in section 4.3 of study Session 4.) They are often used in an attempt to reduce some of the inherent subjectivity of the interview method.

- *Assessment centre* This is a process, rather than a place, which uses a number of selection techniques in combination. Assessment centres have become increasingly popular as a selection method within larger businesses, although they are usually used for more senior positions. They help those selecting candidates to see their abilities from a number of different angles; for example, interpersonal skills in a panel interview or role play exercise, team-working skills in a group activity, IT competence (if appropriate) in a computer simulation.

End note

Some of you may have come across, or even taken part in, the 'manage your own team' competitions usually run online by national newspapers. These involve choosing a 'dream team' for a sport using your knowledge and expertise (or that which you think you have!) as the team's manager. The team you choose is then entered into a 'live' competition where you are playing against other virtual teams in a league. Whoever gets the best results wins the competition. The key point here is that, to be successful in such a competition, you need to think about your team as a whole as well as the individual people within it (as in the business world). You might want to have Maria Sharapova (Russia), Lindsay Davenport (USA), Kim Clijsters (Belgium) and Venus Williams (USA) as the members of your dream women's tennis team, for example, but how will these individuals work together? Will their collective strengths and weaknesses add up to the synergy you require as team manager to get the job done? Choosing the right people and the right team is at the heart of the recruitment and selection process; this is why it almost always involves the line manager and perhaps other members of the team to which the applicant is being recruited.

Maria Sharapova

3.4 Induction and socialisation

A new employee's entry into a business is crucial and, done badly, results in the high costs of the newcomer feeling unhappy, demotivated and unclear about what is expected of them. A poor start to the 'psychological contract' (see study Session 2) is disadvantageous to both sides. The relationship between the business and an employee may begin with the offer of a job and a specific employment contract, but this mutual 'exchange' does not stop there.

Induction and *socialisation* describe different aspects of the process of entry into the business. Induction is usually something quite specific like a short course or meeting the individuals with whom the newcomer will be working. An induction programme is usually short term and includes the more obvious and practical things that can be done to help a new person settle into a job and business; for example, the provision of a job description, health and safety procedures, grievance and discipline policies, and an internal telephone and email directory. Socialisation is more long term and less tangible. It is an ongoing process of understanding in terms of how the newcomer makes sense of the business and their role within it. It is as much about the unwritten rules of the business (often referred to as *organisational culture*) as the formal procedures. Human resource management policies can be thought of as 'clues' as to how the business operates. The criteria used in processes such as recruitment (see section 3.2 in study Session 3) and appraisal (which we look at in study Session 4) set down some expectations, but the way people behave and dress, the structure of meetings and even the size of offices can say something about what the business considers to be important.

Perhaps you have experiences of being inducted into a new role or job? Using Activity 3.4 below, reflect upon the things you did, or what the organisation did, to help you 'fit in'.

Activity 3.4

Spend about **15 minutes** on this activity

Purpose: to consider the process of induction in detail.

Task: think about a recent experience of joining an organisation. This could have been a job in a business but, if not, think about joining a new club or group of friends. Make some notes on the following questions:

1   How did you feel on your first day?

2   What were the key things you felt you needed to know about and the type of support you wished to receive?

Feedback

On your first day did you experience some or all of the following: stress, doubt, lack of self-esteem or confidence, feelings of inadequacy? Alternatively, did you experience a sense of new beginnings: optimism, excitement, anticipation of learning new things? A mixture of emotions is very likely when starting a new job or joining a new group. If, in the first few meetings or days of your job, you were left to 'sink or swim', this should encourage you to think constructively about others' induction and what you could do to help in the future. Your answers to what you needed to know might include a range of factors related to the physical environment, your job role, your colleagues, workplace procedures, and even some apparently trivial details such as where were the toilets and what should you wear.

To make it easier for you to think about the type of information and support that may be useful for a newcomer, it might help to structure the information into different levels, as suggested by Fowler (1996). These are related to a work situation.

- *Individual level* Personal contractual issues and personal support. This could include information on: hours of work and breaks; flexitime arrangements, if any; leave; expenses; payment methods; salary increases and rewards; welfare and other benefits, such as sports and social facilities; training and development opportunities; sickness and absence procedures; geography of buildings and location of facilities; dress code.

- *Job/task level* A general idea of the work to be done and how the employee should make a start. This is likely to include knowledge of: health and safety (for example, fire drills); work procedures (including, for example, security), use of telephones, data protection; other procedures and regulations; equipment and resources available, including IT resources; standards and targets for performance; on-the-job training available; helplines and manuals.

- *Support at departmental level* The relationship of the employee's job to other jobs in the department and to the jobs of people in other departments. This may include: meeting key contacts; defining internal customers; identifying where joint working is required; departmental objectives; departmental communications mechanisms.

- *Organisational level* Wider issues to do with the structure, objectives and wider context of the business as a whole. This could include: policies, aims and core values; HRM policies such as discipline procedures, equal opportunities, staff development and pension and insurance schemes; the structure and functions of the business; the nature and size of the business and its competitors.

These levels assume a large business, but they could be adapted and simplified for small ones. They do not cover everything; additional information may be needed, depending on the particular category of employee and the background and experience of the individual.

3.5 Conclusion

In this study session we have looked at the important 'entry' process of HRM. Securing the right individuals with the right skills for the business does not happen by chance. Making sure that they understand what is expected and that they feel happy that they have made the right choice is crucial in the first few weeks of employment. In the next study session we look at the role of the HRM function in monitoring and assessing people's work.

New recruits at Disneyland undertake a forty-hour apprenticeship programme

3.6 Learning outcomes

By the end of this study session on finding people and helping them fit you should be able to:

- explain recruitment and selection as a two-way process;
- describe the emotive side of recruitment, such as unconscious stereotyping;
- outline the key role of the job description and person specification in recruitment and selection;
- differentiate between induction and socialisation of new employees into a business.

You will have developed your learning by:

- exploring your own potential for stereotyping;
- appreciating how images of certain jobs and professions cause problems for recruitment in certain business sectors.

Session 4 Assessing and developing people at work

Why are we studying 'assessing and developing people at work'?
Employees need a sense of how well they are performing and the opportunity to develop new skills. Achieving the strategic objectives of the business requires some monitoring of current performance and future potential at both the individual and collective level.

The **aims and objectives** of Session 4 are to:

- understand the importance of assessing employees' performance within a business;

- outline some standards of performance;

- explain the process of performance appraisal;

- introduce some methods of, and issues concerning, developing and training people at work.

4.1 Performance management

Ensuring that staff are motivated, pursue common goals, have the knowledge and skills to do their job properly, and can contribute in a meaningful way at work is likely to have an important impact on the overall performance of a business. Conversely, if people are uncertain about their objectives, feel undervalued and demotivated, or cannot influence factors which affect their work, it is likely that performance will suffer. Effective performance will also be dependent on individuals receiving the training and development they need in order to do their jobs well, and on the opportunity to learn new skills and perhaps be moved or promoted into another job. Regular monitoring of work by the HRM department can be used to assess individual performance, address any shortfalls and make the link with rewards where appropriate. Ultimately, the relationship between the performance of the individual and that of the business is linked. This process, called *performance management*, is often claimed to be the most crucial aspect of HRM.

4.2 Assessing performance

The key to managing and developing staff performance is to have a clear idea of what the job holder needs to do to be effective. A number of problems arise if the requirements are vague or ill-defined. For example, the person may lack direction or be working to less than full capacity, and the department and business may not be as productive as they might be. Clarification of what is required is also a central part of appraisal and induction, and the achievement of standards is often linked to rewards and promotion. Example 4.1 below illustrates how one business attempted to enhance employee performance.

'There's still some work left in this one. Get him another pot of coffee.'

Example 4.1

Today many of the most effective organisations view employee performance from an overall corporate and teamwork perspective. For example, South African Breweries (SAB), which has 7000 employees and is placed in the top four breweries in the world, is recognised as a high-performance company in research by the International Federation of Training and Development Organisations.

This achievement is the outcome of a long-term project to raise employee performance and align it with company business strategy. SAB started 'value sharing workshops' in the early 1990s, involving 6000 employees. Out of these, ten key values were established (service, quality, respect, equality, etc.). This was followed by substantial changes in company structure and job design. The emphasis was switched to self-managed, multi-skilled unit and shift teams from conventional hierarchical management and individual working.

To ensure that these changes would be positive there was considerable investment in employee training (which is a continuous programme with an annual spend of 5 per cent of total payroll). The performance standards are maintained through coaching and monitoring being built into team structures and training. In addition, there are monthly individual meetings and six-monthly appraisals, which include upward feedback on managers' performance. Each year a 'people balance sheet' is produced which seeks to measure many elements of company and employee performance such as staffing levels, diversity, competence acquisition, skills gaps.

(Source: based on Johnson, 2000)

Activity 4.1

Spend about **10 minutes** on this activity

Purpose: to highlight commonly used methods of enhancing and measuring employee performance.

Task: reread Example 4.1 above about South African Breweries and some of the methods this business introduced to achieve 'high-performance company' status. Underline key words in the example, compiling a list of methods which were used.

Feedback

The performance enhancement methods utilised by South African Breweries that we found were: workshops, key values, changes in company structure, changes in job design, self-managed teams, multi-skilled units, individual working, investment in training, coaching, mentoring, monthly individual meetings, six-monthly appraisals, upward feedback on managers' performance, and the concept of a 'people balance sheet'. You may have read about other such business performance successes. Look in current newspaper and business magazines for businesses that have been performing particularly well and see if you can spot the type of HRM policies that contributed to this success.

4.3 Setting standards

When talking about standards of performance it is useful to break performance down into different components. For each component it is possible to set appropriate standards to guide the work of the individual, as shown in Table 4.1.

Table 4.1 Standards of performance

Different components of performance and standards, terms and conditions and meeting contractual obligations	Hours of attendance Procedures; for example, notification of sickness absence Adherence to rules of organisation as set out in formal contract
Quality of work	Standards of written work Appearance of finished items of work Acceptable error rates
Work output and timing	Quantity of finished items of work Production norms Deadlines and timescales for completion of work
Interpersonal behaviour and dealing with others	Standards of behaviour in relating to customers/clients Appropriate behaviour in relation to other colleagues and management

Performance standards can be difficult to define and apply consistently. Some aspects of performance lend themselves to the setting of clear quantitative targets, while others may be more subjective and require a qualitative judgement.

Objective quantitative standards of performance

Quantitative standards may involve numerical targets, timescales and deadlines, amounts, costs and resource usage. However, it could be argued that some objectives are not easily described in a single, testable measure. If a customer services manager wants to reward sales staff according to customer satisfaction, they will have to define, develop and test any criteria before using them for managing performance. Another difficulty with objective measures is that they may not be as robust as they appear. Although numerical measures may, on the face of it, seem incontrovertible, further scrutiny may reveal that this is not the case. For example, profitability would seem to be a tried and tested measure, yet accountants know that statements of profit reflect decisions on how to treat costs and revenues and that they can take a creative approach as to what appears in the profit and loss account. In other words, many apparently objective measures are, in reality, quite subjective.

Subjective, qualitative standards of performance

Qualitative standards usually require a more subjective judgement about whether or not they are met. Subjective measures of performance are made in all businesses. Most people have a predetermined picture of the ability and performance of their colleagues that is based only in part on formal output results. These subjective assessments may be useful in deciding who to delegate a task to, who to promote within a department, and so on. Subjective measures are potentially just as important as objective ones, but are associated with a variety of problems. When assessing people subjectively, social influences and personal preferences invariably come into play. It may be that you get on better with a particular person or that you know more about their personal circumstances. Judgements may also reflect ethnicity, gender, appearance or personal biases rather than being based purely on performance.

Feedback on performance

As we saw in study Session 3, well-designed jobs will allow for intrinsic feedback so that individuals can monitor and adjust their own performance. Feedback may include the use and interpretation of data in order to assess, and where necessary to improve, performance. It can be formal or informal and should not be one-way. *Constructive feedback* involves praising strengths and achievements and commenting on areas for improvement, although the emphasis is on suggestions for dealing with difficulties. *Destructive feedback*, meanwhile, focuses on complaining and offers few, if any, positive suggestions.

Whatever performance criteria and standards are used, assessing performance is easier if they are communicated to employees and understood and agreed by them. If employees have been involved in setting targets they will be in a position to assess their own performance and to accept any feedback given. By involving employees in the process, the employer or manager is showing confidence and trust in their abilities – always an important ingredient in motivation.

4.4 Performance appraisal

The appraisal formalises the feedback and performance assessment that has already taken place, looking back and reviewing performance and looking forward to future opportunities. Some form of appraisal system is in use in the majority of businesses, with the formal interview scheduled once or twice a year. Other businesses adopt a less structured approach. Carried out correctly, with planning and in the developmental (not just assessment) spirit intended, performance appraisal is argued to have benefits for all parties.

Table 4.2 The three-way benefits of appraisal

For the individual	For the manager	For the business
Opportunity to encourage staff to review their recent performance and development	Opportunity to motivate staff by recognising achievements	Assistance with succession planning: identifying employees who might be promoted in the future and any development and training they might need
Recognition of the aspects of work they find difficult or irksome, and of contributions that have been appreciated	Chance to clarify and reinforce important goals and priorities so that employees can see precisely where their contribution fits in	Help with workforce planning: identifying areas of strengths and weaknesses in terms of existing skills and development requirement across business
Review and confirmation of agreed goals and standards to be worked to in future	Opportunity to learn about employees' concerns and hopes regarding their current and future roles	Ensuring objectives agreed for groups and individuals harmonise with corporate objectives
Identification of any specific measures to improve current performance (by training, coaching, etc.)	Basis for discussing and agreeing courses of action with employees	Improved communications throughout business
Chance to discuss career aspirations or possible development moves	Clarification of areas of overlap between jobs, improving overall efficiency of team	Above all, improved performance
Improvement of working relationship by increasing communication and understanding		

(Source: based on Evenden and Anderson, 1992, pp. 220–1)

'Before we begin your performance review, I took the liberty of ordering you some comfort food.'

4.5 After assessment: development

One of the major outcomes of an appraisal interview should be agreement on any development needs for the person concerned. We use the term 'development' to describe any experience or process that extends people's skills or abilities. Personal development should increase self-confidence, self-awareness and knowledge, which, if applicable, will contribute to team development. In its turn, the business will benefit from increased skills, greater productivity and the ability of its staff to adapt to change in a positive way.

The responsibility for developing an employee is a shared one. First, the business as a whole has a responsibility to develop policies and provide resources for staff development. In larger businesses this may be embodied in a specialist HRM or training department, the work of which will include identifying commonly occurring training needs, determining cost-effective means of meeting them, monitoring the progress of staff development plans and policies, and advising and assisting line managers in the development of individual staff members. Second, the employee's manager (or team leader or project co-ordinator) has some responsibility. They will know the person's work, previous experience and aspirations and are uniquely placed to assist that person's development. Finally, the individual has an obvious stake in their own development and has to take some responsibility for it. Development is not something you can 'do' to people: they must make it their own or it will not happen.

Not thinking about staff development on an ongoing basis is short-term thinking for a business, given that its purpose is to raise the level of skills and standards overall. Imagine that an insurance company employs someone initially to do basic clerical tasks such as looking after the post, photocopying and switchboard duties. Over a period the employee is supported through a business administration and IT vocational qualification, and the job role expands to take on more IT tasks and becomes secretarial rather than just general office work. On top of this, the person is encouraged to attend a customer service course and on return to work they take on more people-related duties. Through careful planning, based on a consideration of future needs, the individual has developed and other people in the business benefit too.

A caution: development is not always the answer

Inexperience and lack of training are far from being the only causes of the problems that people face in businesses. Consider the following situations:

- Staff say the work is too difficult and they do not stay. Is this because they lack sufficient training and support, or is too much being expected of them?

- There is constant friction between two teams. Is this because the team leaders have not really come to terms with the demands of their management responsibilities; or does the friction arise from overlapping responsibilities and inadequate procedures?

- The staff group is trying to develop a non-hierarchical way of working, but there have been some serious mistakes (with clients being left waiting for hours) and confusion in dealings with suppliers. Does this indicate that the staff should have some sessions on team working (with a trainer or with staff from another business that has more experience of this way of working)? Or is this form of collective working impractical with such a large group? Perhaps they would do better to have a co-ordinator role that they rotated.

Another classic mistake is to imagine that training and development can make people competent in work for which they are temperamentally unsuited, or for which they do not have an aptitude. This is common in young, growing businesses, and in periods of rapid change. The result is a person doing a job that they would never have been recruited for, had managers in the business known how things would develop.

4.6 Development is not just training courses

An important distinction between different kinds of training and development is the relative degree of formality that they entail. Formal development includes internal and external training courses of different types, and specific, formalised on-the-job learning; informal development includes experiences such as mentoring, coaching and job rotation.

There is a range of options available, depending on the size of the business, the number of people involved and the complexity of what it is that needs to be learnt. They are:

- *coaching:* a way of transferring knowledge and skill from a more experienced person to a less experienced person;

- *mentoring:* is similar to coaching, but the person carrying out the mentoring should not be the other person's line manager;

- *job rotation:* encouraging members of a team to be able to work proficiently in each other's jobs, thus creating greater flexibility and skills within the team as a whole;

- *special assignments/projects:* increasing the skills base of individuals by arranging supervised project work in preparation for greater responsibilities;

- **action learning**: a group of individuals who work on their own chosen problems, but share advice and approaches to solving each other's problems;

- *'in-house' courses*: a means of conveying knowledge and skills to groups of individuals through training (provided either from within the business or by external trainers).

- *courses provided by external agencies*: to convey knowledge or skills to groups of individuals, for example by specialist trainers or through attendance at a local college.

- *distance learning*: a course such as this one.

4.7 Different approaches to training and development

Businesses, even within the same sector, may take very different approaches to training and developing their staff. Smith and Hyton (1999), in a survey of 1,760 enterprises in Australia, found that training activity tended to be triggered by specific operational factors, such as the introduction of new technology, rather than by strategic issues. Other factors that influenced the provision of training were:

- the size of the business
- the business sector in which it operated
- government policy
- senior managers' commitment to training
- the occupation of the employee.

Becherman et al. (1997), following a study of Canadian organisations, identified three patterns which characterised the different ways in which businesses appear to make decisions relating to training:

1 incidental learning

2 event-triggered training

3 commitment to the learning organisation.

These are considered briefly below.

Incidental learning

The business decides not to make any formal investment in training, but instead training takes place through informal, on-the-job learning. This approach to training is linked to an inward-looking business strategy and low labour turnover, which means that the business sees no need for formal training. When training takes place, it is in response to a specific demand, such as provision of health and safety practice.

Event-triggered training

The business undertakes training as and when a specific event, such as work reorganisation, requires it. Training in this case is an episodic activity which is used systematically to provide solutions to particular problems.

Commitment to the learning organisation

The business has made continuous learning an integral part of its strategy. Senior management believes that training, employee involvement and motivation are critical and complementary parts of business success.

What type of training and development works best for you? If you haven't already completed the reflective activities in the Study Companion connected with this book, do so now!

4.8 Conclusion

Having secured the right person for the job, this investment has to be monitored and developed. Clarity of purpose for both employer and employee is essential through recruitment, acclimatisation/socialisation, ongoing assessment of performance and maintenance of standards. This study session has introduced many new ideas; what is clear once again, though, is that HRM is a perpetual and dynamic process, helping people to attain their best levels of performance on behalf of the business for which they work. In the next section we look at some of the broader issues concerning HRM.

4.9 Learning outcomes

By the end of this study session on assessing and developing people at work you should be able to:

- describe some methods and standards used in the measurement of performance at work;

- outline the benefits of performance appraisal;

- explain the importance of the development of employees within a business and describe the different methods that could be used.

You will have developed your learning by:

- reflecting on the methods of enhancing and measuring employee performance using an actual business case (Activity 4.1 and Example 4.1 on South African Breweries).

Session 5 HRM in a wider context

Why are we studying 'HRM in a wider context'? It is difficult to imagine any aspect of business that does not involve and have an impact upon people. In this final study session, we look at the development of the concept of HRM and look at HRM from alternative perspectives, including the point of view of the 'insiders': the employees who experience it.

The **aims and objectives** of Session 5 are to:

- introduce the professional body for HRM in the UK: the Chartered Institute of Personnel and Development;
- consider the differences between HRM being the responsibility of a specialist function and that of line managers within a business;
- compare the characteristics of what are termed 'hard' and 'soft' HRM;
- describe some theoretical models of HRM;
- reflect on some of the more controversial aspects of HRM.

5.1 The emergence of HRM

As we discovered in the earlier study sessions of this book, the emergence of HRM has mirrored the changing needs and expectations of both businesses and employees. There is a long history of attempts to try to understand how people behave at work. As welfare policies and work procedures developed, so the business function of personnel management was born. From humble roots, it has developed into a recognised area of management practice. One way of illustrating the growth and importance of this business function is to take a look at the Chartered Institute of Personnel and Development (CIPD), the professional body responsible for the HRM profession in the UK.

5.2 The Chartered Institute of Personnel and Development

The ***Chartered Institute of Personnel and Development*** is the professional body for those involved in the management and development of people. Its ethos, qualifications and practices are based on a set of professional standards which the next activity invites you to explore.

Activity 5.1

Spend about **1 hour** on this activity

Purpose: to find and access the Chartered Institute for Personnel and Development (CIPD) website and view some current HRM issues underlying professional standards.

Task: go now to the CIPD website. The link is given in the B120 online resources or you can type 'CIPD' into Google, Yahoo! or a similar search engine. On the CIPD home page you can see the contents of its web pages, including the current HRM headlines and issues. Now enter the term, 'professional standards' into the search box at the top right-hand corner. You can now explore the different types of standards and what they mean. Make notes on the standards and what you think of them. If you have time left over, explore the parts of the CIPD website that are of most interest to you, but the main focus of the activity is on the professional standards section.

Feedback

All professions have a set of standards that underpin their professional qualifications and entry to the profession.

The establishment of these skills and competencies, as they are often called, is crucial in maintaining standards and consistency. As you will have found by completing Activity 5.1, the CIPD define their standards as shown below.

Professional Standards

One of our key objectives is to establish, monitor and promote standards and ethics for the profession.

Our Professional Standards cover the whole spectrum of personnel and development, taking into account generalist and specialist functions. Using the concept of the thinking performer[*], they define the levels of knowledge and competence you need to demonstrate when operating at a support or practitioner level or as an advanced practitioner. They govern entry to CIPD membership and act as a benchmark for the profession.

[*]The 'thinking performer' concept and vision underlines our Professional Standards. Our qualifications and levels of membership give members the resources they need to encourage their employees to become 'thinking performers'.

(Chartered Institute for Personnel and Development, 2006)

As reflected in the CIPD standards, one of the key principles of an HRM approach is that all line managers in the business are involved with HRM issues. Indeed, as Marchington and Wilkinson observe:

… a thread running through all the standards … is that P&D [personnel and development] specialists need to be able to *gain line management commitment* for their proposals and recommendations. It matters little that a course of action impresses other P&D specialists if it fails to convince line managers – the people who have to put most P&D policies into effect. This is not to say that P&D specialists should become the servants of line managers, merely recommending what the line managers want to hear in order to gain 'customer' approval. But it does meant that P&D specialists need to be acutely aware of their audience, of the purpose of human resource policies, and their contribution to organisational success. On some occasions the existing views of line managers will need to be challenged and the basis for their perspectives questioned, whilst on others their needs will have to be met with a professional judgement and sound practical advice.

(Marchington and Wilkinson, 1996, p. 3)

The next section focuses on the differences between line managers and a central HRM department dealing with people matters within a business.

5.3 Involving line managers in HRM

As business times have changed, so have the activities of the personnel/ HRM function. In the 1970s, for example, the prominence of trade unions meant that industrial relations was an important part of the role. A cynical view is that the change of name from personnel to HRM is only that: a change of name; but the immense literature that has grown around HRM since the 1990s argues that it is a completely different way of perceiving and dealing with the workforce within a business (see, for example, Storey, 2001). The key challenge of an HRM approach is that businesses integrate people issues at a strategic level. That is, the implications for the workforce in terms of how many people to recruit, what skills they are to be trained in, how they are to be rewarded, and so on, are primary considerations in any business decisions. The degree to which this can be achieved will inevitably vary according to the size, history, culture and product of each business. Within small businesses, for example, it is usually the owner or a particular individual who will be responsible for HRM, probably dealing with people issues as they arise. In larger businesses there is likely to be a dedicated HRM department made up of specialists. Increasingly, however, HRM issues will tend to be devolved to line managers. This is a key aspect of the HRM approach: that it is the individual managers who work with employees on a day-to-day basis who will know best about the kind of person required for the job and the best ways to motivate them.

Activity 5.2

Spend about **10 minutes** on this activity

Purpose: to consider the advantages and disadvantages of devolving HRM issues to individual line managers.

Task: consider the suggestions given in Table 5.1 below regarding the possible advantages and disadvantages of (a) HRM professionals and (b) line managers being responsible for dealing with people issues within a business. Add any further advantages and disadvantages you can think of.

Feedback

The advantages and disadvantages listed here, and the ones you may have thought of, centre around the *objectivity* of HRM specialists and the *subjectivity* and 'hands-on' involvement of line managers. Both have their strengths; a combination of both may be best but, of course, in the majority of businesses (that is, small, with relatively few employees) there will not be a dedicated HRM department. Approaches to dealing with people issues in a business may have as much to do with culture and values as with established HRM procedures. You might wish to reflect on whether this is (a) true or (b) a good thing.

Table 5.1 HRM in the hands of specialists versus line managers

	Advantages	Disadvantages
HRM specialists	Could provide a more objective assessment in recruitment or performance appraisal	Removed from day-to-day observation and knowledge of individual employees
	Broader view of HRM procedures and policies	Perceived as a bureaucratic nuisance
	'On-tap' HRM services with dedicated time to spend on HRM matters	Large amounts of employment data to gather and process
Line managers	Direct contact with and knowledge of employees	Dealing with paperwork involved could be very time consuming
	Immediate approach to problems	Need to learn and update people-management skills

5.4 Hard and soft HRM

One continuum that is used in the HRM literature to capture these different 'shades' of HRM is that of 'hard' or 'soft'. Neither is right in itself: it depends on the business, and the approach may well be a mix of the two or somewhere in between.

Under the 'hard' HRM approach, the key objectives would be to:

- carefully delineate written contracts of employment;
- monitor performance closely;

- offer controlled access to training courses;
- set formal rules and monitor adherence to them;
- implement managerial decisions for the workforce;
- construct regularised pay scales;
- have collective bargaining contracts (if unions are present).

Under the 'soft' HRM approach, HRM managers would see their role as:

- working with individual contracts of employment;
- utilising **performance-related pay** schemes;
- encouraging team work;
- treating the selection and recruitment of employees as an integral, key task within the business strategy;
- using facilitative and participatory approaches in decisions making;
- being alert to employees needs for motivation, flexibility, and so on.

(Based on Storey, 1995, p. 10)

These different types of approaches to HRM will vary according to the individual business and probably the culture and traditions of the sector and country in which it is situated. In section 5.5, which includes Essential Reading 1, we look at some of the well-known models of HRM.

5.5 Academic models of HRM

The Harvard model of HRM (1981)

Human resource management was introduced as a subject of academic study at Harvard Business School in the USA in 1981. This came about because the teaching staff felt that recent developments in the academic areas of personnel, organisational behaviour, labour relations and organisational development demanded a new course. The Harvard model of HRM, as it is known, is reproduced in Figure 5.1.

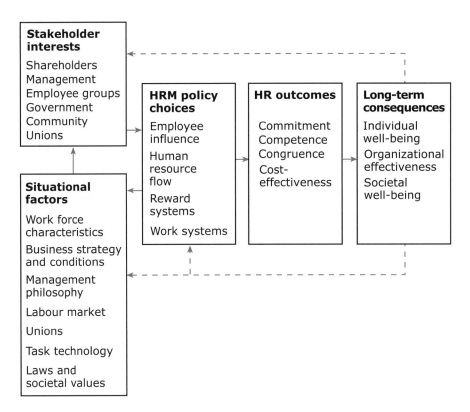

Figure 5.1 The Harvard model of HRM (Source: *Managing Human Assets* by Michael Beer, Bert Spector, Paul R. Lawrence, D. Quinn Mills, Richard E. Walton. Copyright © 1984 by The Free Press)

The conceptual overview shown in Figure 5.1, mapping the 'territory of HRM', emphasises the close connection between the HRM function and both the internal and external environments of the business. The stakeholders' interests and situational factors (factors which make up the context in which the business operates) are interlinked with HRM policy choices which in turn lead to HRM outcomes. These outcomes have implications for stakeholder interests and situational factors, and so on. The effectiveness of the business is represented in the model as a critical long-term (and necessary) consequence, but this is placed alongside individual and societal well-being. A business utilising this approach to HRM would have to ensure that its employees were involved in their work and able to participate in decision making.

The Michigan model of HRM (1984)

The Harvard model can be compared with another famous and founding model of HRM produced by Fombrun et al. in 1984. This is known as the Michigan model of HRM and is reproduced in Figure 5.2.

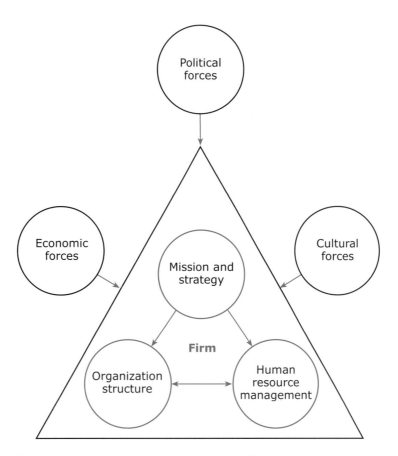

Figure 5.2 The Michigan model of HRM (Source: *Strategic Human Resource Management* by C. J. Fombrun, N. M. Tichy, and M. A. Devanna (Fig. 3.1, p. 35), copyright © 1984 John Wiley & Sons)

Use the following activity to stop and think about what has been said about the two HRM models described so far and to learn about Guest's UK-focused (as opposed to US-focused) model of HRM.

Differences between the two models

It can be suggested that the Harvard model is an example of 'soft' HRM because it concentrates attention on the outcomes for people. Note the inclusion of the factors of well-being and commitment to the business in Figure 5.1. The Michigan model can be described as a model of 'hard' HRM because it emphasises the business treating employees as a means to achieving strategy. Increasing productivity is viewed as the main reason for having the HRM function. People become a resource that is used in a calculated and rational way, with the needs of the business being paramount. Both these models are American and it can be argued that they reflect American cultural traditions, management styles, politics and industrial relations.

Activity 5.3

Spend about **1 hour** on this activity

This activity is based on Essential Reading 1, taken from an introductory HRM textbook by Ashly Pinnington and Tony Edwards (2000). It is intended to reinforce your understanding of some of the most famous models of HRM and clarify the difference between 'hard' and 'soft' HRM as introduced above. Please note that this is an essential reading, not an additional (optional) one, which means that we think it is extremely useful to your study and understanding of the subject and it is therefore counted in your study hours for this book. Please also note that two of the figures in Essential Reading 1 are the same as Figures 5.1 and 5.2 in this section. They have been included within the main text here as well as in Essential Reading 1 in order to enhance your understanding of two important academic models of HRM.

Purpose: to reinforce your understanding of some key ideas within the field of HRM.

Task: read Essential Reading 1, 'North American and British models of HRM', by Ashly Pinnington and Tony Edwards, which you will find at the back of this book. Read it carefully and, as always, make notes as you go along. Ask your tutor about anything you don't understand, or raise it as a question in your online tutor group forum. Use the following questions to check that you have picked up the main points of the reading:

1 What are the four categories of the Harvard model?

2 What does 'employee influence' mean in this model?

3 What are the 'four Cs' in the Harvard model?

4 Why is the Harvard model categorised by Pinnington and Edwards as being an example of 'soft' HRM?

5 What are the four main outcomes of Guest's British model?

6 In what ways is Guest's model different from the Harvard model?

7 What is claimed to be the main strength and limitation of the Michigan model?

8 Why is the Michigan model categorised by Pinnington and Edwards as being an example of 'hard' HRM?

Feedback

We haven't provided the usual feedback section for this activity because we want you to complete the reading. It is an essential reading and study time has been allocated to it. The questions above are intended to ensure that you have understood and made notes on the key points in the reading.

5.6 HRM: A controversial issue?

Although the HRM phenomenon has usurped personnel management as an approach to managing people in many businesses, it remains a highly controversial issue for some. There are still numerous questions about its nature, its meaning and its application. These questions are important because they relate to how HRM is linked to business strategy and the kind of people-management policies and practices that are implemented in a business. We take a brief look at two of these questions below: the possibility of strategic integration and the ethical dimension of HRM.

Is strategic integration possible?

A central implication of HRM is that people management is linked to business strategy. Related to this is the notion that the various people-management policies and practices that a business operates should be coherent and consistent in order to help deliver business strategy. It is debatable how the fit between business strategy and HRM strategy, policy and practice – known as external integration – might be best achieved. The kind of rational analysis necessary to deliver an HRM strategy and to formulate HRM policy and practice is likely to be subverted by the political interests of the various parties involved, many of whom may wish to resist change in order to protect their own power base (Mabey et al., 1998). It is not surprising, therefore, that evidence for the uptake of HRM generally indicates a piecemeal, rather than a strategic, approach.

For example, consistency and coherence of HRM policies and practices – internal integration – are considered to be important factors in determining whether or not HRM 'fits' with business strategy. This implies that the range of HRM practices that a business operates is mutually supportive – for example, that performance appraisal is linked to training and development. In fact, evidence suggests that, while there is fairly extensive use of individual elements of HRM, far fewer businesses succeed in linking these practices together in a meaningful strategic way (Storey, 2001). Gratton et al. (1999), for example, found that, while the businesses they studied *espoused* a coherent HRM strategy, there was little actual evidence of this strategy being translated into coherent HRM practice. They concluded that their findings indicated a mismatch between HRM theory and HRM practice, in that how HR managers described HRM practice was quite different from how this practice was perceived by employees. In particular, while many of the businesses they studied espoused the 'commitment' *rhetoric*, their behaviour was in fact perceived as controlling by their employees who frequently demonstrated low levels of commitment.

The ethical dimension of HRM

It has been argued that, given the nature of human resources, they have to be managed with reference to some kind of ethical framework. Ethics has been defined as 'the consideration and application of frameworks, values and principles for developing moral awareness and guiding behaviour and action' (Winstanley and Woodall, 2000, p. 43). Clearly, there are ethical implications in a range of HRM policies and practices, such as recruitment and selection, performance appraisal, reward and equal opportunities. For example, managers' bias in favour of certain individuals (due to friendship, gender or ethnic background) may dispose them to give these people preferential treatment, compared with other equally able colleagues.

Dimensions of HRM, such as flexibility, commitment and performance management, raise other ethical issues. Flexibility in terms of short-term contracts may imply less job security. Demonstration of commitment may mean that individuals are obliged to work long hours, even though they may not wish to do so. Performance-related pay may mean that employees have less certainty about their financial security. It is clear, therefore, that decisions relating to the management of people should be subject to some kind of ethical consideration. Winstanley and Woodall (2000) argue that best practice of HRM is not on its own sufficient to ensure the ethical treatment of individuals at work. In order to achieve this, they suggest that HRM policy and practice must be underpinned by a 'human-centred' perspective, derived from ethical sensitivity and reasoning.

5.7 'Mischief' at work

Another aspect of work that can challenge the implementation of HRM policies is 'organisational mischief'.

All businesses have a visible (or formal) and less obvious (informal) side. Some things can be quite easily controlled and structured (for example, office space, pay structures) and some things cannot (for example, attitudes, chemistry between individuals). Businesses are made up of people and, while we might want to be able to manoeuvre them like human resources, we must always retain a note of scepticism about whether this is either possible or desirable. 'Unofficial' aspects of working in a business need not be negative (although some are, such as sabotage, harassment, absenteeism, pilfering, bullying); rather, they are just inherent aspects of human behaviour. They may happen as a direct challenge to authority, such as instigating a 'go-slow' on a production line and inciting unrest amongst fellow employees. However, they may have more to do with the boredom of the work or a feeling that one's 'psychological contract' (see study Session 1) is unfair. In agreeing to work for the business, one is implicitly agreeing to commit to it in some way, to adhere to what is acceptable, to surrender a certain amount of personal autonomy, if only by having to turn up at the workplace and complete certain tasks. This often hidden aspect of life in a business has clear consequences for the HRM function. One way of thinking about it is as 'organisational mischief' which can be defined as: 'Activities occurring within the workplace that (a) according to the official structure, culture, rules and procedures of the organisation "should not happen" and (b) contain an element of challenge to dominant modes of operating or to dominant interests in the organisation' (Watson, 2002, p. 346).

No matter how well structured individual, team and business objectives may be, it is always possible to make it difficult for others at work. Some psychological satisfaction is likely to be gained from 'throwing a sickie' once in a while (taking an unauthorised day off work claiming sickness), or from merely playing a practical joke on a newcomer or manager. The induction rituals of young apprentices are well known: trainee motor mechanics, for example, are often asked to go to the parts department and ask for a 'long stand'. They are kept waiting quite a while! For those employees working directly with customers, ways to 'get one's own back' on difficult or rude characters include ignoring their gestures for attention, short changing them or 'spoiling' the food or drinks being served to them (disgusting, but unfortunately not uncommon). Humorous pranks occur between employees, and then there is the nastier politicking: another inherent and inevitable aspect of groups of people working together. We can probably all think of individuals we know who demonstrate what could be described as 'naked ambition': socialising only with the people at work who can further their career. Many comedy situations are built on this premise; for example, some of you may remember the nice but weak Jerry, husband of Margo in the marvellous BBC comedy *The Good Life* in the 1970s.

The four main characters from the BBC comedy, *The Good Life*

Laughing at work is probably an important emotional outlet. It can be seen in humorous documents and emails passed around a business, or in the signs on noticeboards and individuals' work stations, such as 'you don't have to be mad to work here but it helps' and 'the floggings will stop when morale improves'. For students of business, the point here is that the policies and approach of the HRM function may be to blame for levels of 'mischief' at work becoming unacceptable. It could be interpreted as a collective call for more interesting work, more involvement in decisions, and more communication about what is going on.

5.8 Conclusion

The HRM function will always be central to any business because it deals with issues regarding people, the core element. In this study session we have looked at some of the activities that an HRM function (or representative in smaller businesses) would be involved in. However, we have given equal space to some of the broader issues and 'alternative' perspectives we might use to consider whether the implementation of HRM policies can be as straightforward as some business texts suggest.

5.9 Learning outcomes

By the end of this study session on HRM in a wider context you should be able to:

- outline the idea behind professional standards in HRM;
- explain the difference between 'hard' and 'soft' approaches to HRM;

- compare the situations of having specialists or line managers responsible for HRM in a business;
- describe the main aspects of the Harvard, Michigan and Guest models of HRM.

You will have developed your learning by:

- accessing the CIPD website and navigating through to specific pages;
- considering the issues involved in devolving HRM to the line managers within a business.

Conclusion to Book 2

While HRM is only one functional area of a business, what happens there is likely to have implications across the business. Developing from largely administrative personnel activities to an integral part of what most line managers do in a business, HRM has become an established academic subject within business studies. We have seen how the different academic models which attempt to explain and predict the relationship between employer and employee have been developed over recent decades. Because the management of people is more unpredictable than the management of some other resources, there will always be both a controversial and a subjective side to HRM. It is as much about how people understand what is happening in the business and in their own roles as about what is actually taking place. We hope that this placing of HRM in a wider context has reinforced your understanding and fired your enthusiasm for the subject.

References

Arnold, J., Coombs, C. R., Wilkinson, A. J., Loan Clark, J., Park, J. R. and Preston, D. (2003) *Looking Good? The Attractiveness of the NHS as an Employer to Potential Nursing and Allied Health Professional Staff: A Report Prepared for the Department of Health Based on Research Conducted as Part of the Human Resources Initiative*, Final Report, May, Loughborough, Loughborough University Business School.

Arnold, J., Cooper, C. L. and Robertson, I. T. (1995) *Work Psychology: Understanding Human Behaviour in the Workplace* (2nd edn), London, Pitman.

Becherman, G., Leckie, N. and McMullen, K. (1997) *Developing Skills in the Canadian Workplace: The Results of the Ekos Workplace Training Survey*, Ottawa, Canadian Policy Research Networks.

Buchanan, D. A. and Preston, D. (1992) 'Life in the cell: supervision and teamwork in a "Manufacturing Systems Engineering" environment', *Human Resource Management Journal*, Vol. 2, No. 4, pp. 1–25.

Buchanan, D. and Huczynski, A. (1991) *Organizational Behaviour: An Introductory Text* (2nd edn), Hemel Hempstead, Prentice Hall.

Buchanan, D. and Huczynski, A. (2004) *Organizational Behaviour: An Introductory Text* (5th edn), Harlow, Prentice Hall.

Chartered Institute for Personnel and Development (2006) *Professional Standards* [online] http://www.cipd.co.uk/mandq/standards/default.htm?IsSrchRes=1 (accessed 19 April 2006).

Coombes, R. (2005) 'Be prepared for a surprise', *Guardian, Society*, 16 February [online] http://society.guardian.co.uk/children/story/0,,1415016,00.html (accessed 17 October 2005).

Cooper, C. L. (2000) *Theories of Organizational Stress*, Oxford, Oxford University Press.

Evenden, R. and Anderson, G. (1992) *Making the Most of People*, Wokingham, Addison Wesley.

Fombrun, C. J., Tichy, N. M. and Devanna, M. A. (1984) *Strategic Human Resource Management*, New York, John Wiley & Sons.

Fowler, A. (1996) *Employee Induction: A Good Start*, London, Institute of Personnel and Development.

Gratton, L., Hope Hailey, V., Stiles, P. and Truss, C. (1999) *Strategic Human Resource Management: Corporate Rhetoric and Human Reality*, Oxford, Oxford University Press.

Guest, D. (2001) 'Industrial relations and human resource management' in Storey, J. (ed.) *Human Resource Management: A Critical Text*, London, Thomson Learning.

Hackman, J. R. and Oldham, G. R. (1980) *Work Redesign*, Reading, MA, Addison Wesley.

Hattenstone, S. (2004) 'Lucky for some', *Guardian*, 6 November [online] http://www.guardian.co.uk/lottery/story/0,,1344308,00.html (accessed 19 April 2006).

Johnson, R. (2000) 'The beverage report', *People Management*, Vol. 6, No. 7, pp. 28–37.

Maccoby, M. (1988) *Why Work: Motivation and Leading the New Generation*, New York, Simon and Schuster.

MacErlean, N. (2000) 'Pulling the rug under the "sickie": absenteeism is a national disease', *Observer, Business*, 20 August, p. 14.

Marchington, M. and Wilkinson, A. (1996) *Core Personnel and Development*, London, Institute of Personnel and Development.

Maslow, A. (1943) 'A theory of human motivation', *Psychological Review*, Vol. 50, No. 4, pp. 370–96.

McGregor, D. C. (1960) *The Human Side of Enterprise*, New York, McGraw Hill.

Pinnington, A. and Edwards, T. (2000) *Introduction to Human Resource Management*, Oxford, Oxford University Press.

Price, A. (2004) *Human Resource Management in a Business Context* (2nd edn), London, Thomson.

Roberts, K. H. and Glick, W. (1981) *The Job Characteristics Approach to Task Design: A Critical Review*, Berkeley, CA, University of California.

Smith, A. and Hyton, G. (1999) 'What drives enterprise training? Evidence from Australia', *International Journal of Human Resource Management*, Vol. 10, No. 2, pp. 251–72.

Steers, R. M. and Rhodes, S. R. (1978) 'Major influences on employee attendance: a process model', *Journal of Applied Psychology*, Vol. 63, No. 4, pp. 391–407.

Storey, J. (ed.) (1995) *Human Resource Management: A Critical Text*, London, Routledge.

Storey, J. (ed.) (2001) *Human Resource Management: A Critical Text* (2nd edn), London, International Thomson Business Press.

Taylor, F. W. (1911) *The Principles of Scientific Management*, New York and London, Harper.

Trist, E. L. and Bamforth, K. W. (1951) 'Some social and psychological consequences of the longwall method of coal-getting', *Human Relations*, Vol. 4, No. 1, pp. 3–38.

Tyler, S. (2004) *The Manager's Good Study Guide*, Milton Keynes, The Open University.

Vroom, V. H. (1964) *Work and Motivation*, New York, John Wiley.

Ward, L. and Inman P. (2005) 'Nine-to-five in decline as UK embraces flexi-time', *Guardian*, 5 July, p. 8.

Watson, T. J. (2002) *Organizing and Managing Work*, Harlow, Prentice Hall/ Pearson Education.

Wignall, A. (2005) 'Rise: a firm beginning', *Guardian*, *Rise*, 8 October, p. 2.

Winstanley, J. and Woodall, D. (2000) *Ethical Issues in Contemporary Human Resource Management*, London, Macmillan.

Essential Reading 1

North American and British models of HRM

Soft HRM

The Harvard Model, Beer *et al.* (US)

HRM was launched as a course in 1981 at Harvard Business School. It was the first new course in Harvard's core curriculum to be introduced for nearly twenty years. It was established because there was widespread feeling among Harvard's faculty that new developments in the fields of organisational behaviour, organisational development, personnel administration, and labour relations were best represented in a new course. In 1985, Richard Walton published an article in the *Harvard Business Review* called 'From Control to Commitment in the Workplace', which popularized soft HRM as a distinctive approach to managing human resources. His argument was that effective HRM depends not on strategies for controlling employees but on strategies for winning employees' commitment. The Harvard model, first put forward in 1984 by Michael Beer *et al.* in the book *Managing Human Assets*, takes a soft HRM perspective similar to that of Walton and was devised primarily to inform general managers of improved ways of managing people. The model recommends that general managers must hold greater responsibility for HRM. How to get general managers more involved in HRM has been a major preoccupation for organisations in the 1980s and 1990s and so we now consider Beer's model in more detail rather than Walton's which concentrates on the mutual concerns of employers and employees.

The Harvard model proposes that many of the diverse personnel and labour relations activities can be dealt with under four human resource (HR) categories: employee influence, human resource flow, reward systems, and work systems.[1] These are general issues that managers must attend to regardless of whether the organisation is unionized or not, whatever management style is applied, and whether it is a growing or declining business.

Employee influence is the question of how much responsibility, authority, and power is voluntarily delegated by management and to whom. One of the critical questions here is, if management share their influence, to what extent does this create compatibility (the word the authors used is 'congruence') of interests between management and groups of employees? The assumption the authors make is that any influence employees have should be compatible with management's purpose and priorities. *Human resource flow* concerns managing the flow of people into, through, and out of the organisation. This means making decisions on recruitment and selection, promotion, termination of employment, and related issues of job security, career development, advancement, and fair treatment. Managers and personnel specialists, according to the Harvard model, must work together to ensure that the organisation has an appropriate flow of people to meet its strategic requirements.

Reward systems regulate how employees are extrinsically and intrinsically rewarded for their work. Extrinsic rewards are tangible pay and benefits: pay, overtime pay, bonuses, profit sharing, pensions, holiday entitlement, health insurance, and other benefits, such as flexible working hours. Intrinsic rewards are intangible benefits and are said to strongly influence employees' motivation, job satisfaction, and organisational commitment. Intrinsic rewards are rewards from the work itself, such as sense of purpose, achievement, challenge, involvement, self-confidence, self-esteem, and satisfaction. The Harvard model recommends that employees should be highly involved in the design of an organisation's reward systems but observes that final decisions, besides meeting employees' needs, must be consistent with the overall business strategy, management philosophy, and other HRM policies. *Work systems* are the ways in which people, information, activities, and technology are arranged, at all levels of the organisation, so that work can be performed efficiently and effectively.

Policies in these four areas must be designed and applied in a coherent manner because, Beer and his co-authors argue, HRM is considerably less likely to be effective where policies are disjointed, made up of odd combinations of past practices, and are *ad hoc* responses to outside pressures. The four policy areas must satisfy the many stakeholders of the enterprise – for example, shareholders, employees, customers, suppliers, communities, trade unions, trade associations, and government. Employees are major stakeholders of the enterprise and it is the responsibility of managers to establish systems that promote employee influence. Some people would say that managers do not consider enough how to facilitate employee influence; indeed, Beer *et al.* claim that, of the four issues discussed, employee influence is the central feature of an HR system, as illustrated in the triangle in Fig. R1.1.

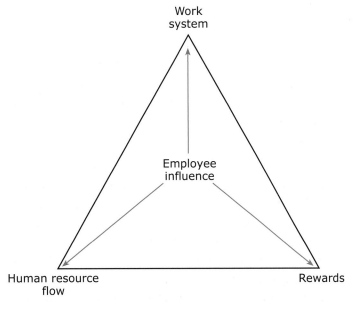

Figure R1.1 Human resource system (*Source: Managing Human Assets* by

Michael Beer, Bert Spector, Paul R. Lawrence, D. Quinn Mills, Richard E. Walton. Copyright © 1984 by The Free Press.)

A further recommendation of the Harvard model is that, when making HRM policy decisions, managers should consider the 'four Cs': commitment, competence, congruence (compatibility), and cost-effectiveness. That is, managers should ask to what extent the policies they implement will: enhance the *commitment* of people to their work and the organisation; attract, retain, and develop people with the needed *competence*; sustain *congruence* (compatibility) between management and employees; and be *cost-effective* in terms of wages, employee turnover, and risk of employee dissatisfaction.

The authors' conceptual overview of HRM is represented diagrammatically as a 'map of the HRM territory' (see Fig. R1.2). They propose that HRM is closely connected with both the external environment and the internal organisation. Their model of the territory of HRM shows that stakeholder interest and 'situational factors' (the factors that make up the context in which a business must operate) are interlinked with HRM policy choices, which in turn lead to HR outcomes. These outcomes have long-term consequences that have a feedback effect on stakeholder interests and 'situational factors', and so on. The main stakeholder interests are: shareholders, management, employee groups, government, the community, and unions. The situational factors are: workforce characteristics, business strategy and conditions, management philosophy, labour markets, unions, task technology, and laws and societal values. The long-term consequences of HR outcomes are considered under three main headings: individual well-being, organisational effectiveness, and societal well-being.

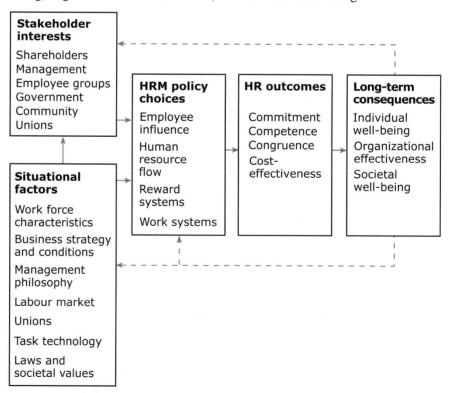

Figure R1.2 A map of the HRM territory (*Source: Managing Human Assets* by Michael Beer, Bert Spector, Paul R. Lawrence, D. Quinn Mills, Richard E. Walton. Copyright © 1984 by The Free Press.)

The Harvard model is soft HRM because it concentrates attention on outcomes for people, especially their well-being and organisational commitment. It does not rank business performance or one of the stakeholder interests – for example, shareholders – as being inherently superior to other legitimate interests, such as the community or unions. Organisational effectiveness is represented in the Harvard model as a critical long-term consequence of HR outcomes, but alongside the equally important consequences of individual and societal well-being. An organisation putting this model into practice would therefore aim to ensure that its employees were involved in their work and able to participate in decision making. HRM policies would be developed and implemented to meet employees' needs for influence, but within the limitation of having to be consistent with the overall business strategy and management philosophy.

Guest (UK)

A second soft HRM model came from David Guest in 1987.[2] Guest argued that HRM in the UK should be about designing policies and practices to achieve four main outcomes: strategic integration (planning/implementation); high employee commitment to the organisation; high workforce flexibility and adaptability; and a high-quality workforce. Strategic integration means ensuring that the organisation's business plans are implemented through appropriately designed HR polices and practices. Companies have been criticized for treating HRM and strategy separately, therefore failing to combine HRM with the business strategy.

He proposed that these four HRM outcomes will lead to the desirable organisational outcomes of high job performance, stronger problem solving, greater change consistent with strategic goals, and improved cost-effectiveness, while also reducing employee turnover, absences, and grievances. However, Guest warned that these outcomes will be achieved only if an organisation has a coherent strategy of HRM policies fully integrated into the business strategy and supported by all levels of line management.

Guest's model is similar to the Harvard but has seven HR policy categories instead of four (see Fig. R1.3). Four of Guest's categories are broadly the same as Beer's Harvard categories. Where Beer has *human resource flow*, Guest has *manpower flow* and *recruitment, selection,* and *socialization*; both models have *reward systems* as a category; and what Beer calls *work systems* Guest calls *organisational and job design*. Guest's three other categories are: policy formulation and management of change; employee appraisal, training, and development; and communication systems.

Policy formulation and management of change means establishing HR policy to explicitly identify the nature of the change required in a business and manage the process of change. *Employee appraisal, training, and development* involve both informally and formally evaluating employee performance and the need for training and development. Once these have been evaluated, policies must be in place to ensure that timely and appropriate training and employee development occur. *Communication systems* are the various processes and media that the organisation uses to encourage two-way flows of information between management and employees. Typically, these systems use bottom-up and top-down methods: a bottom-up method might be, for example, an employee suggestion scheme, and a top-down method might be a quarterly newsletter on the business performance of the organisation.

Policies for identifying human resource and organisational outcomes

Policies	Human resource outcomes	Organisational outcomes
Organisational and job design		High job performance
Policy formulation and implementation/ management of change	Strategic planning/ implementation	High problem-solving
Recruitment, selection and socialization	Commitment	Successful change
Appraisal, training and development	Flexibility/adaptability	Low turnover
Manpower flows – through, up and out of the organization		Low absence
Reward systems	Quality	Low grievance level
Communication systems		High cost-effectiveness i.e. full utilization of human resources

Figure R1.3 Guest's model of HRM

Source: Guest, D. E., 'Human Resource Management and Industrial Relations', *Journal of Management Studies* (1987), 24, 5, September, pp. 503–21, Table 11, p. 516.

Guest's model has been criticized for presenting an ideal and for assuming unrealistic conditions for practising HRM.[3] Guest himself reported ten year later, in 1997, that whilst considerably more research data on HRM in organizations had been gathered, the link between the adoption of HRM policies and high performance remains somewhat elusive. He described progress in the UK towards HRM as being somewhat slow and 'crab-like'. British trade unions, he wrote, have started to become more positive about HRM and will work more openly and productively with management; however, many senior managers still retain a short-term perspective on their businesses. The result is that many HR initiatives appear to employees to be management fads rather than a genuine long-term commitment to the organization and its people.

Guest's model constitutes soft HRM for the same reasons that the Harvard model does: both give strong recognition to the needs of employees (for example, motivation and development) in the running of the organization. Also, both are committed to employees' needs as long as the measures taken to meet those needs remain consistent with the strategy of the organization and management aims. Guest claims his model is more straightforward than the Harvard model, which maps the territory of HRM, because he simply prescribes that improved implementation of just seven HR policies will result in better HR outcomes.

Hard HRM

The Michigan Model, Fombrun *et al.* (US)

In the same year (1984) that Beer *et al.* published *Managing Human Assets*, Fombrun, Tichy, and Devanna published *Strategic Human Resource Management*.[4] This book proposed a different model of HRM, frequently referred to as the Michigan School because one of its main proponents was an academic from the University of Michigan's Graduate School of Business Administration,[5] although the ideas were generated in partnership with researchers from two other well-known American universities, Wharton and Columbia. The British academic, John Storey, describes this model as 'hard' HRM because it emphasizes treating employees as a means to achieving the organization's strategy, as a resource that is used in a calculative and purely rational manner. Hard HRM focuses more than soft HRM does on using people as resources and as a means towards the competitive success of the organization.[6]

It is easy to be overly simplistic when evaluating Fombrun, Tichy, and Devanna's approach to HRM. On the one hand, there are those who dismiss it for being inhuman; on the other, there are those who proclaim it to be just common sense and the only route to business success. Arguably, the strength *and* the major limitation of their approach is that it focuses on the organization and how it can best rationally respond to its external environment. Focusing on the level of the organization has the advantage of drawing attention to aspects partly under the control of management, such as formal strategy, structure, and preferred culture. On the other hand, attending to the organizational level may lead managers to assume that, through organizational strategy, structure, and HR systems, they have more power than they really have to change individuals and influence the external environment.

Hard HRM assumes that increasing productivity will continue to be management's principal reason for improving HRM; while this is a major factor in many private- and public-sector organizations, it clearly is not the only one. Fombrun *et al.* argue that conditions of the external environment – for example, heightened competition and market uncertainty – necessitate 'strategic' HRM, that is, HRM designed to achieve the strategies, or goals, of the organization.

The authors proposed a framework for strategic HRM that assumes the needs of the firm are paramount.[7] They said organizations exist to accomplish a mission or achieve objectives and that strategic management involves consideration of three interconnected issues. First, the mission and strategy must be considered because these are an organization's reason for being. Second, the organization's structure, personnel requirements, and tasks, must be formally laid out, including systems of accounting and communications. Third, HR systems need to be established and maintained because, as the authors state, 'people are recruited and developed to do jobs defined by the organization's formal structure: their performance must be monitored and rewards allocated to maintain productivity'.[8]

The Michigan model observes that different business strategies and related organization structures can lead to contrasting styles of HRM in activities such as selection, appraisal, rewards, and development.[9] For example, a single-product company with a traditional functional structure (that is, structured according to the various functions of the business – finance, accounting, marketing, sales, production and operations, personnel, etc.) will select its people on the basis of their expertise in the specific functions. Appraisal of employee performance will be largely informal and administered via personal contact; the reward system will vary unsystematically across the functions and employee development will be limited primarily to the functional area in which the employee works. On the other hand, a company with a multi-divisional structure and a strategy for product diversification may have a very different system of HRM. Selection would be systematic and according to both functional experience and general management ability. The appraisal system would be formal and impersonal based on quantitative criteria such as productivity and return on investment and on qualitative, subjective judgements about individual performance. The reward system would systematically reward contribution to the diversification strategy, and bonuses would likely be paid according to achievement of profitability targets. Employee development would be more complex and systematic than it would be in a company with a single-product strategy. In the multi-divisional company, employees are accustomed to being periodically transferred to different functions and areas of business. Individual development would be cross-divisional, cross-subsidiary, and corporate.

The Michigan model represents the external and internal factors of HRM as a triangle (see Fig. R1.4). Once management have decided how the mission and business strategy, organization structure, and HRM are to be organized and integrated – and assuming it is an appropriate response to political, economic, and cultural forces – then they can begin to design the human resource system in more detail.

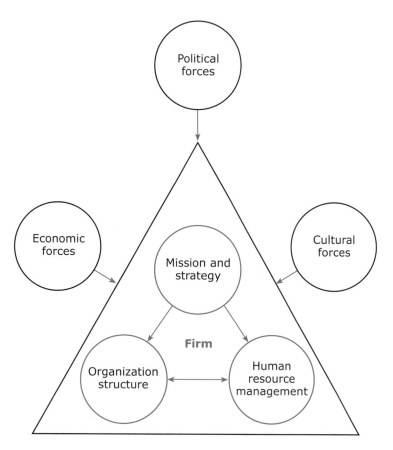

Figure R1.4 Strategic management and environmental pressures *(Source: Strategic Human Resource Management* by C. J. Fombrun, N. M. Tichy, and M. A. Devanna (Fig. 3.1, p. 35), copyright © 1984 John Wiley & Sons.)

Performance is a function of all the human resource components: *selecting* people who are best able to perform the jobs defined by the structure, *appraising* their performance to facilitate the equitable distribution of rewards, motivating employees by linking *rewards* to high levels of performance, and *developing* employees to enhance their current performance at work as well as to prepare them to perform in positions they may hold in the future.[10]

Finally, the Michigan model argues that within HRM there is a human resource cycle affecting individual and organisational performance (see Fig. R1.5). It describes the four functions of this cycle as follows:

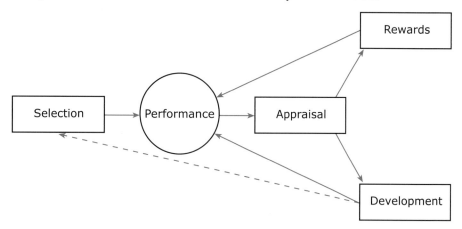

Figure R1.5 The human resource cycle (*Source: Strategic Human Resource*

Management by C.J.Fombrun, N.m. Tichy, and M.A. Devanna (fig 3.2, p. 41), copyright ©1984 John Wiley & Sons.

The Michigan model is hard HRM because it is based on strategic control, organisational structure, and systems for managing people. It acknowledges the central importance of motivating and rewarding people, but concentrates most on managing human assets to achieve strategic goals. Subsequent empirical research has not produced evidence of organisations systematically and consistently practising hard HRM, although a longitudinal study (by Truss *et al.*, 1997) of large organisations (including BT, Citibank, Glaxo, Hewlett Packard, and Lloyds Bank) found that employees were managed by tight strategic direction towards organisational goals. A company practising hard HRM would have a style of management that treats employees in a calculated way, primarily as [a] means to achieving business goals. Its top management would aim to manage the organisation rationally and achieve a 'fit' between the organisation's strategy, structure, and HRM systems.

Notes

1 Beer, M., Spector, B., Lawrence, P. R., Quinn Mills, D., Walton, R. E., *Managing Human Assets* (New York: The Free Press, 1984). Beer, M. and Spector, B., 'Corporate wide transformations in human resource management', in R. E. Walton and P. R. Lawrence (eds.), *Human Resource Management – Trends and Challenges* (Boston, Harvard Business School Press, 1985). It should be noted that the actual term 'soft HRM' was coined later by John Storey in 1988.

2 Guest, D. E., 'Human Resource Management and Industrial Relations', *Journal of Management Studies* (1987), 24, 5, pp. 503-21. Truss *et al.* (1997) [Truss, C., Gratton, L., Hope-Hailey, V., McGovern, P., and Stiles, P., 'Soft and Hard Models of Human Resource Management: A Reappraisal', *Journal of Management Studies* (1997), 34, 1, January pp. 53–73] argue that Guest's model actually combines hard and soft HRM, the primary hard element being strategic integration.

3 Bratton, J. and Gold, J., *Human Resource Management: Theory and Practice* (Basingstoke: Macmillan, 1994), pp. 23–6; Keenoy, T., 'HRM: Rhetoric, Reality and Contradiction', *International Journal of Human Resource Management* (1990), 1, 3, pp. 363–84; Keenoy, T., 'HRM: a case of the wolf in sheep's clothing?', *Personnel Review* (1990), 19, 2, pp. 3–9.

4 Fombrun, C. J., Tichy, N. M., and Devanna, M. A., *Strategic Human Resource Management* (New York: John Wiley & Sons, 1984).

5 Legge, K., *Human Resource Management: Rhetorics and Realities* (Basingstoke: Macmillan, 1995).

6 Storey, J., 'Developments in the management of human resources: an interim report', *Warwick Papers in International Relations* (University of Warwick, November, 1987); Storey, J., *Developments in the Management of Human Resources* (Oxford: Blackwell, 1992); Beardwell, I. and Holden, L., *Human Resource Management: A Contemporary Perspective*, 2nd edn (London: Financial Times, Pitman Publishing, 1997).

7 Devanna, M. A., Fombrun, C. J., and Tichy, N. M., 'A Framework for Strategic Human Resource Management', in C. J. Fombrun, N. M. Tichy

and M. A. Devanna, *Strategic Human Resource Management* (New York: John Wiley & Sons, 1984), pp. 33–51.

8   Ibid., p. 34.

9   Fombrun *et al.* (pp. 36–9) developed their concept of HRM through discussion of some of the well-known literature on management style, organisational structure, and strategy, notably Mayo (1933) [Mayo. E., *The Human Problems of an Industrial Civilisation* (New York: Macmillan, 1933)], Chandler (1962) [Chandler, A. D., *Strategy and Structure: Chapters in the History of the American Industrial Enterprise* (Cambridge, MA: MIT Press, 1962)], and Galbraith and Nathanson (1978) [Galbraith, J. R. and Nathanson, D., *Strategy Formulation: Analytical Concepts* (St. Paul, MN: West Publishing Company, 1978)].

10 Devanna *et al.*, 'A Framework for Strategic Human Resource Management', p. 41.

(Source: Pinnington, A. and Edwards, T., 2000, *Introduction to Human Resource Management*, Oxford, Oxford University Press, pp. 6–14.)

Acknowledgements

Grateful acknowledgement is made to the following sources for permission to reproduce material in this book:

Text

Example 1.2: MacErlean, N., 'Pulling the rug under the "sickie": absenteeism is a national disease', *Observer*, 20 August 2000. Copyright Guardian Newspapers Limited 2005; *Example 3.3:* Coombes, R., 'Be prepared for a surprise', *Guardian*, 16 February 2005. Reprinted with permission from the author; *Example 3.4:* Wignall, A., 'Rise: a firm beginning', *Guardian*, 8 October 2005. Copyright Guardian Newspapers Limited 2005; *Essential Reading 1:* Pinnington, A. and Edwards, T. (2000) *Introduction to Human Resource Management*, Oxford University Press.

Figures

Figure 1.1: from Maslow (1954) in Tyler, S. (2004) *The Manager's Good Study Guide*, Milton Keynes, The Open University, p. 262, Figure 13.3; *Figure 1.2:* Steers, R. and Rhodes, S. (1978) *Journal of Applied Psychology*, Vol. 63, APA Journals; *Figure 2.1:* Hackman and Oldham (1980), sourced in Arnold, J. et al., (1995) *Work Psychology: Understanding Human Behaviour in the Workplace*, Pitman Publishing; *Figures 5.1, R1.1 and R1.2:* Beer, M. et al. (1984) *Managing Human Assets*, Copyright © by The Free Press; *Figures 5.2, R1.4 and 1.5:* Fombrun, C., Tichy, N. and Devanna, M. (1984) *Strategic Human Resource Management*. Copyright © 1984 John Wiley & Sons; *Figure R1.3:* Guest, D. E. 'Human resource management and industrial relations', *Journal of Management Studies*, No. 24, 5 September 1987.

Photographs/Illustrations

Page 9: www.JohnBirdsall.co.uk; *Pages 15 and 49:* © Randy Glasbergen; *Page 18:* © Photick – Image and Click/Alamy; *Page 25:* © Image Source/Alamy; *Page 26:* © Mike Baldwin/www.CartoonStock.com; *Page 27:* reproduced with permission from Roy Export Company Establishment; *Page 28:* © Royalty-Free/Corbis; *Page 34:* Blend Images/Alamy; *Page 36:* © FRAN/www.CartoonStock.com; *Page 39:* © BananaStock/Alamy; *Page 41:* © Rex Features; *Page 45:* © Paul Thompson Images/Alamy; *Page 47:* © Ted Goff; *Page 53:* © Image Source/Alamy; *Page 63:* © Blend Images/Alamy; *Page 64:* © BBC, courtesy of the BBC.

Cover

Front cover image: Medio Images/Fotosearch Stock Photography and Stock Footage.

Module team

B120 team

Dr Anja Schaefer
Dr Nik Winchester
Dr Warren Smith
Dr Vira Krakhmal
Barry Jones, *Curriculum Manager*
Carey Stephens
Susan Hughes
Rosie McGookin
Val O'Connor, *Curriculum Assistant*

The original course team

Dr Diane Preston, *Course Team Chair*
Patricia McCarthy, *Course Manager*
Dr Kirstie Ball
Penny Marrington
Fran Myers
Dr Anja Schaefer
Dr George Watson
Rita Gregory, *Course Team Assistant*
Val O'Connor, *Course Team Assistant*

Other contributors

Professor Judy Day
Dr Lorna J. Eller
Mick Fryer
Jonathan Winship

External examiner

Kate Greenan, *Professor of Management Education and Head of School of Accounting, Ulster University*

Developmental testers

Linda Fisher
Adam Messer
John Messer
Marina Ramtohul

Critical readers

Patricia Coffey, *Senior Lecturer, University of Brighton Business School*
Clare Cromarty, *OUBS Associate Lecturer*
Patricia Dawson, *Principal Lecturer, Thames Valley University, retired*

Helen Higson, *Director of Undergraduate Studies, Aston Business School*
Beverly Leeds, *Principal Lecturer, University of Central Lancashire*
Jill Mordaunt, *OUBS Senior Lecturer*
Nigel Walton, *OUBS Associate Lecturer*

Production team

Martin Brazier, *Graphic Designer*
Angela Davies, *Media Assistant*
Richard Dobson, *Editor*
Hannah Eiseman-Renyard, *Editor*
Diane Hopwood, *Rights Assistant*
Lee Johnson, *Media Project Manager*
Siggy Martin, *Assistant Print Buyer*
Katy Nyaaba, *Media Assistant*
Jill Somerscales, *Editor*

The original production team

Holly Clements, *Media Assistant*
Lene Connolly, *Print Buyer*
Jonathan Davies, *Graphic Designer*
Julie Fletcher, *Media Project Manager*
Fiona Harris, *Editor*
Diane Hopwood, *Compositor*
Kate Hunter, *Editor*
Jon Owen, *Graphic Artist*
Deana Plummer, *Picture Researcher*
Dave Richings, *Assistant Print Buyer*
Jill Somerscales, *Editor*